THE SPREAD OF PRINTING

EDITED BY COLIN CLAIR

SOUTH AFRICA

THE SPREAD OF PRINTING

EASTERN HEMISPHERE

South Africa

by

ANNA H. SMITH

1971
AMSTERDAM: VANGENDT & CO
LONDON: ROUTLEDGE & KEGAN PAUL
NEW YORK: ABNER SCHRAM

ISBN 90-6300-025-1

Commonwealth of Nations
ROUTLEDGE & KEGAN PAUL LTD LONDON
7100-6477-2

North America
ABNER SCHRAM (SCHRAM ENTERPRISES LTD) NEW YORK
8390-0025-1

Library of Congress Catalog Card Number 72-78403

Set in Monotype Bembo Series 270
Koninklijke Drukkerij G. J. Thieme N.V., Nijmegen
Printed in the Netherlands

Preface

This essay is, as far as is known, the first attempt to sketch the introduction of printing and its development to the beginning of the twentieth century in the whole of Southern Africa. Consequently there are a number of unsolved problems and numerous omissions. Moreover, the text was written in 1967, and names such as South African Public Library and Department of Education, Arts and Science have become obsolete. The oldest library in South Africa is now called the South African Library, Cape Town; and the Department has been divided into two, namely the Department of Cultural Affairs and the Department of Higher Education. There is no reference in this work to recently discovered information about some of the mission presses or to articles on South African printing which appeared in periodicals since 1967. Nevertheless, it is believed that nothing of great importance has been omitted, and it is therefore hoped that by bringing together information scattered throughout many published and unpublished sources, this volume in the series, *The Spread of Printing*, may help to bring to light not only hitherto unknown details about individual printers and their presses, but also examples of their publications which have so far eluded the bibliographers.

Finally, I wish to thank the Publishers for all the trouble they have taken in seeing this essay through the press.

Anna H. Smith

Johannesburg
17 March 1969.

Contents

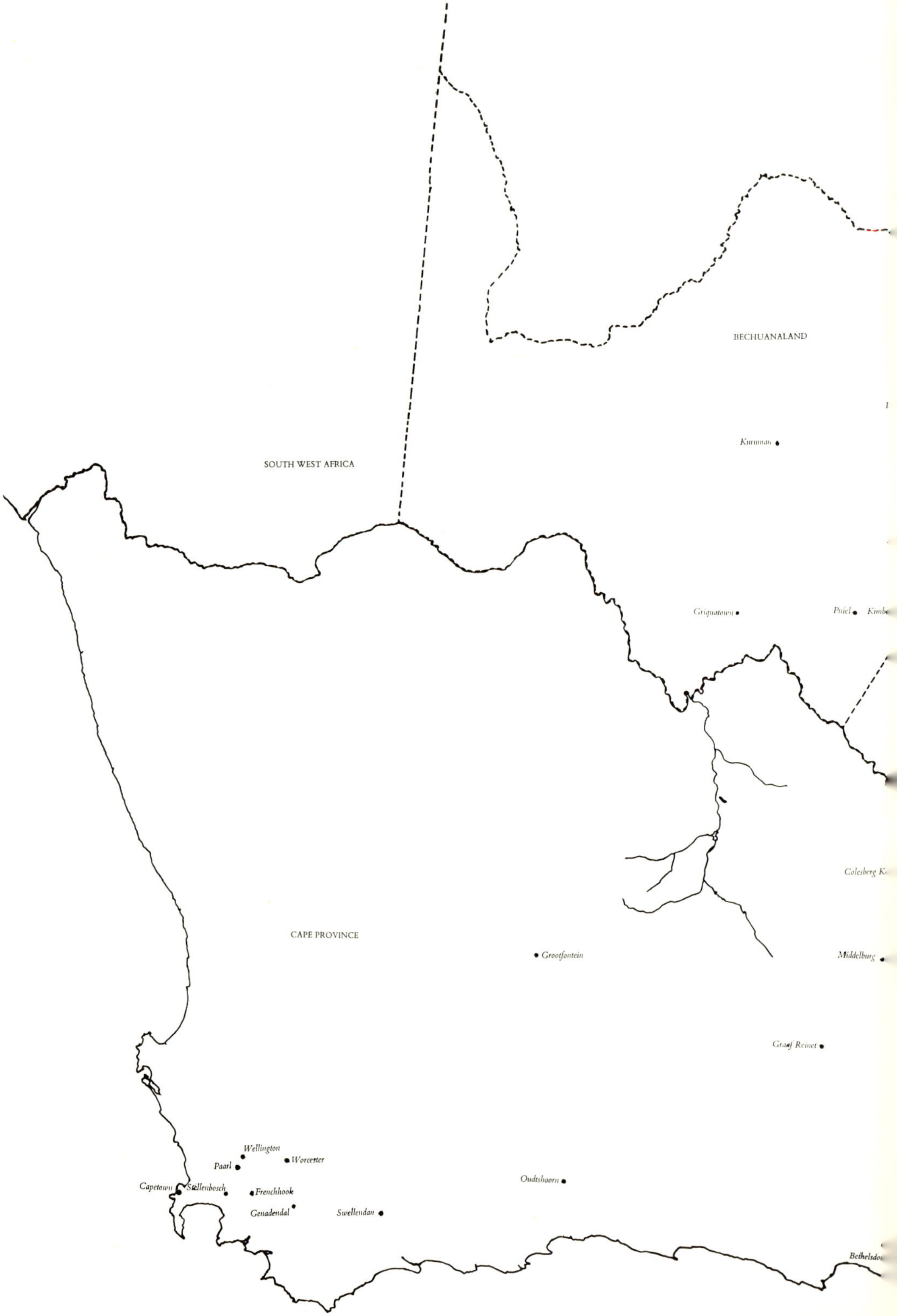
SOUTH WEST AFRICA
BECHUANALAND
Kuruman
Griquatown
Pniel
CAPE PROVINCE
Grootfontein
Colesberg
Middelburg
Graaf Reinet
Oudtshoorn
Wellington
Worcester
Paarl
Capetown
Stellenbosch
Frenchhook
Genadendal
Swellendan

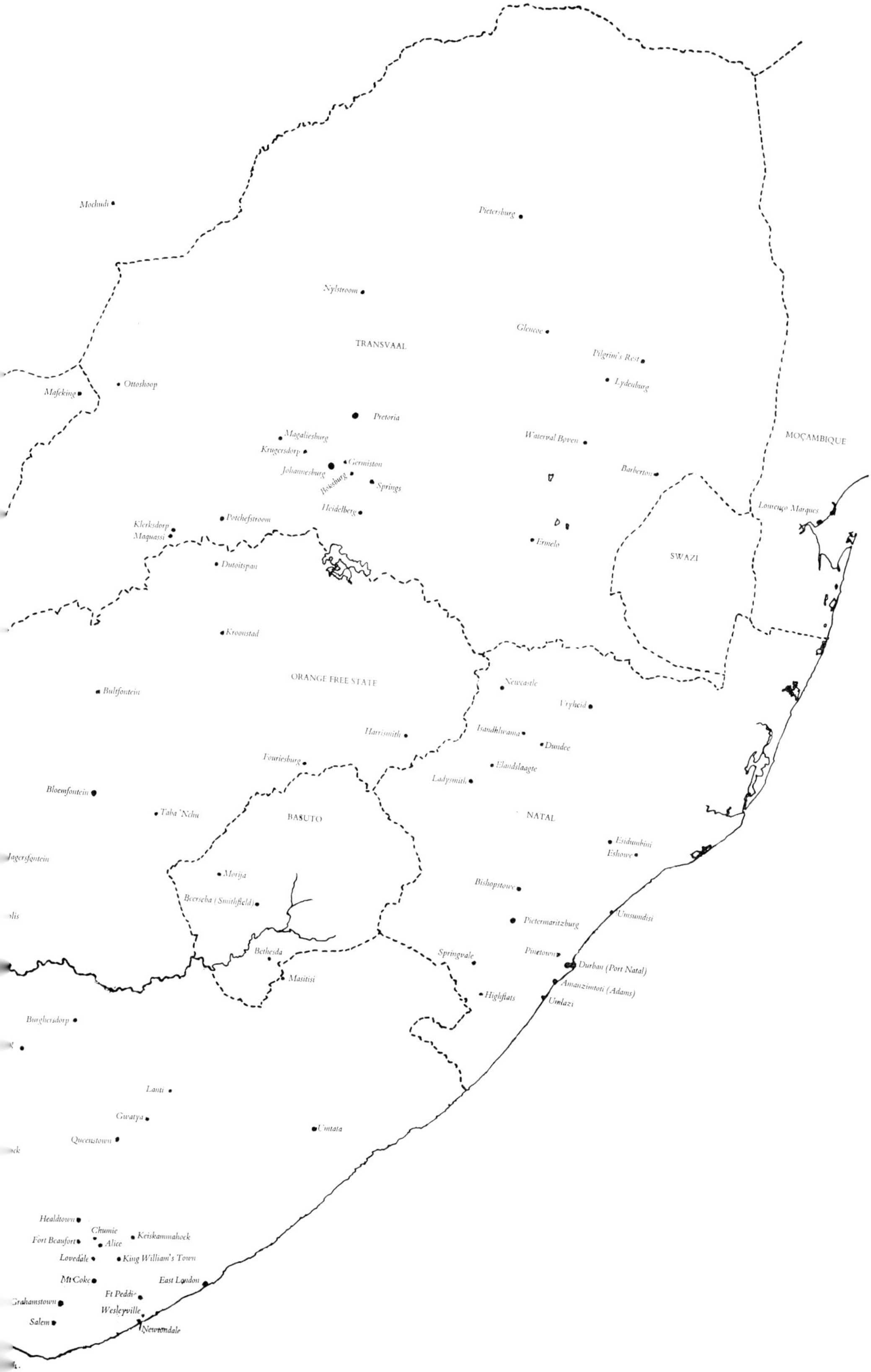
Mochudi
Pietersburg
Nylstroom
TRANSVAAL
Glencoe
Pilgrim's Rest
Lydenburg
Mafeking
Ottoshoop
Pretoria
Magaliesburg
Krugersdorp
Johannesburg
Germiston
Boksburg
Springs
Waterval Boven
MOÇAMBIQUE
Barberton
Heidelberg
Lourenço Marques
Klerksdorp
Maquassi
Potchefstroom
Ermelo
SWAZI
Dutoitspan
Kroonstad
ORANGE FREE STATE
Bultfontein
Newcastle
Vryheid
Harrismith
Isandhlwana
Dundee
Fouriesburg
Elandslaagte
Ladysmith
Bloemfontein
Taba 'Nchu
BASUTO
NATAL
Esidumbini
Eshowe
Morija
Bishopstowe
Beerseba (Smithfield)
Umsundisi
Pietermaritzburg
Bethesda
Springvale
Pinetown
Durban (Port Natal)
Masitisi
Amanzimtoti (Adams)
Highflats
Umlazi
Burghersdorp
Lanti
Gwatya
Umtata
Queenstown
Healdtown
Chumie
Keiskammahoek
Fort Beaufort
Alice
Lovedale
King William's Town
Mt Coke
East London
Ft Peddie
Wesleyville
Salem
Newtondale

SOUTH AFRICA

	km²		square miles	
Approximate total area		5,077,000		1,960,300
Cape Province	717,000		277,000	
Natal and Zululand	91,000		35,400	
Orange Free State	130,000		50,400	
Transvaal	289,000		111,200	
Republic of South Africa		1,227,000		474,000
Basutoland (Lesotho)		26,000		10,300
Bechuanaland (Botswana)		582,000		225,000
Swaziland		17,000		6,500
South West Africa		843,000		322,400
Rhodesia		384,000		148,600
Portuguese East Africa		760,000		293,500
South of Zambezi	375,000		145,000	
North of Zambezi	385,000		148,500	
Angola		1,243,000		480,000

All values approximated into round figures

The Beginnings in Cape Town

When the Portuguese discovered the route to India round the Cape of Good Hope towards the end of the fifteenth century, none of the peoples with whom they came into contact on the shores of Africa south of the Zambezi River had any tradition of writing or printing. The first European settlement in South Africa was established by the Dutch East India Company in Table Bay in April 1652 as a half-way house between Holland and the East. The Cape station was established for the express purpose of providing fresh supplies and medical services to the passing ships, and the Lords Seventeen, the highest authority of the Company, were anxious that the settlement should be run on the most economical lines and with as little trouble as possible. Jan van Riebeeck, who was in command for ten years, was instructed to keep the usual official manuscript diary of daily occurrences in the settlement, but more than a century was to pass before any mention of a printing press occurs in the records.

The Cape remained in the hands of the Dutch East India Company from 1652 until 1795, when the British occupied it and kept it until 1803. This period is known as the First British Occupation. The Dutch East India Company had by this time become defunct, and when Britain, under the treaty of Amiens (1802), restored the Cape to the Dutch, it was not to the Company but to the Government, known as the Batavian Republic of the Netherlands. The Batavian Republic was in control of the Cape only from 1803 to 1806, when the British took over after the engagement at Blaauwberg near Cape Town. This became a permanent arrangement in 1814, when a treaty was signed in London, by which it was agreed that Britain should retain the Cape and pay the Netherlands compensation.

In 1779 the burghers or colonists, as the settlers had come to be called, sent four men to Amsterdam to deliver in person, to the Lords Seventeen, a petition concerning their grievances. The interview took place on 16 October, and article 7, on proposed measures for improving the situation, included a request for the establishment by the Company of a printing works and the appointment of a printer, so that authentic copies of laws, official instructions, rules, and regulations could be made generally available to the colonists.[1] Although Governor J. van Plettenberg supported Article 7, the Lords Seventeen on 3 December 1783 decided that they would have sufficient copies of official documents printed and sent to the Cape. In other words the request of the Cape colonists for a local printing press was turned down. According to A.C.G. Lloyd's pioneer work 'The Birth of Printing in South Africa' which was originally published in *The Library* of January 1914, and in revised form in *South African Libraries* in July 1933, Governoi C. J. van de Graaff, who succeeded Van Plettenberg, referred to his predecessor's request for a printing press for the use of the authorities at the Cape, and on 7 February 1786 he stated that the only way to keep abreast of the work of copying the increasing number of official documents was to install a press and to have some of the clerks taught to print. He was of the opinion that the authorities should control the press to prevent abuse.

Again in 1792, when the officials at the Cape were asked to reduce the number of people employed in copying official documents, the Council of Policy suggested that a printing press run on lines similar to those in force in Batavia would be the best method of resolving the problem. It was suggested that the press should be under the direct supervision of the Secretary of the Council of Policy and be situated in the Castle for the sake of security and proper supervision.[2] The book-binder in the employ of the Cape, Johan Christiaan Ritter, was consulted in the matter, and on 3 December 1792 a list of equipment for a complete printing office (drawn up by Ritter) was sent to the Lords Seventeen. On 28 June 1794 this body sent a letter to the Cape sanctioning the proposals and the list of items required. They added instructions that the press was to be housed in the Castle, that it was to be used solely for the Company's official business, and that Ritter was to be put in charge.

Johan Christiaan Ritter was born in Hof on the River Saale in Germany on 25 July 1755 as the second son of the book-binder Georg Stephan Ritter and his wife Johanna Dorothea, born Leidenfrost. The *Archives Year Book for South African History*, vol. 9, issued in 1946 (p. 339) includes details about Ritter collected from the documents in the Cape Town Archives, by Dr. J. Hoge, who categorically states that

1. Beyers, C. *Die Kaapse Patriotte, 1779–1791*. Kaapstad, Juta, pref. 1929, p. 28.
2. Boeseken, A. J. 'Die Nederlandse Kommissarisse en die 18de Eeuse Samelewing aan die Kaap' in *Archives Year Book for South African History*, vol. 7, 1944, p. 135.

Ritter 'brought a hand printing-press with him', while D. H. Varley writing on 'An Early Cape Printing Discovery' in the *Quarterly Bulletin of the South African Library*, v. 1, no. 1, Sep. 1946, p. 9, a little more cautiously, mentions 'the small hand affair brought out by J. C. Ritter, or received shortly after his arrival, as book-binder to the Dutch East India Company, in 1784'. So far no contemporary evidence concerning the source of Ritter's press has been found, and some writers have suggested that he made use of the press they surmise must have been available for making the paper money authorized in 1782. But as notes circulated at this time have not survived, it is impossible to say whether a press was needed, or whether it would have been possible to use this particular press for ordinary printing. The latei notes which have survived are not printed. As no details of a technical nature about Ritter's press are known today, the possibility that it was a crude affair locally made at the Cape cannot be entirely excluded. Judging by the following petition addressed by Ritter to Sir George Yonge, the Governor of the Cape, on 20 August 1800, the press was presumably still in the book-binder's possession at this date:

Humbly Sheweth

That your Excellency's Petitioner has been Bookbinder to Government these sixteen years and has during all that time practised printing such Trifles as his small apparatus would allow, so as to recommend him to the notice of the former Government who, having proposed him to the Directors of the dutch India Company, were there upon authorised, that, as soon as the necessary Materials for a printing press could be sent here, Your Excellency's Petitioner was then to commence acting as managing Printer to Government.

That, as in the mean while this Colonij was surrendered to the arms of His Majesty, and the aforesaid arrangement could not, therefore, be effected. Your Excellency's Petitioner has continued as Bookbinder to Government as well as printing, as aforesaid, trifling things, among which there were, during three years, small Almanacs calculated after the Meridian of this place, but having successively been applied to bij sundrij persons, naij even by Secretarij Ross, for larger performances, which his Materials at hand would not, however, allow, ijet being encouraged bij these applications to enlarge that business, has written to Europe for a printing apparatus on a much larger scale, which was to enable him to print anijthing that might be required either by Government or bij anij Individual.

That, having now seen Your Excellencij's Proclamation forbidding everij person from printing anijthing, Your Excellencij's Petitioner, feeling highlij distressed more especiallij on account of the said printing-apparatus & Materials, which he has every reason to apprehend is on the eve of it's arrival here, and which cannot now be of any use to him, therefore takes the liberty most respectfully to applij to Your Excellencij and most humblij to praij, that it maij please Your Excellencij graciouslij to assist him in this his distress, either by ordering the whole of his abovementioned printing Tools and Materials to be purchased of him, like those of Mr. Smith, by the

Printers to Government or in such another manner as Your Excellency in Your paternal benevolence, will think proper.

And Your Excellency's Petitioner
as in duty bound shall ever pray

Exhibited
the 20 August 1800.

Ritter[1]

Of 'the tiifles' mentioned by Ritter as being printed at the Cape before 1800, hardly anything has survived, except a fragment of one leaf of the Almanac for 1796, which is preserved in the South African Public Library, Cape Town. Much has been written about this scrap of paper, but nothing definite is known of its provenance. The picture on the title-page (?) was probably from an imported block and gives the impression of having been engraved. Some of the lettering on this page does not look like type either. The reverse, very crude, was probably printed with movable type at the Cape. Some writers have suggested that type must have been available at the Cape because bank-notes were locally produced. No notes dating from before 1800 which have survived show any signs of having been printed—they are embossed and have signatures and other information in manuscript. In addition to binding official documents for the Company, Ritter is on record as having had to *stamp* the letters received and despatched as well as the paper money. As he was employed as an engraver of seals as well, it is small wonder that he complained of having too much to do and asked for additional assistants.[2] Whether he compiled the almanacs on his own initiative or on instructions from the Company, is not known. It is believed that almanacs were issued in 1795, 1796, and 1797. Two more or less contemporary references to these almanacs exist, and both are a little malicious. Sir John Barrow was an official during the period of the first British Occupation of the Cape and closely associated with Andrew Barnard, Colonial Secretary at the Cape, whose wife, Lady Anne, was responsible for the second comment. Barrow[3] states that 'no printing-press has yet found its way to the Cape of Good Hope, except a small one for cards or handbills. They contrive, indeed, to publish a sort of almanac, but that of the current year [1796 or 1797?] has somewhat suffered in its

1. Cape Archives Document BO 32, p. 463–464.
2. Hoge, J. 'Personalia of the Germans at the Cape, 1652–1806' in *Archives Year Book for South African History*, vol. 9, 1946, p. 339.
3. Barrow, John. *An Account of Travels into the Interior of Southern Africa in the years 1797 and 1798.* London, T. Cadell & W. Davies, 1801, vol. 1, p. 377.

reputation, by having stated an eclipse of the moon to fall on the day preceding the full, and to be invisible, when, unluckily for the almanac-maker, it happened at the proper time, visible, and nearly total.'

Lady Anne Barnard[1] on 1 June 1800 wrote as follows about the almanacs. 'The printer made a fortune of two shillings by it: each of the four districts took one at sixpence—all the inhabitants read or copied out of that one.'

Exactly when in 1784 Ritter arrived at the Cape is not recorded, but some authorities say it was in the second half of the year. Before 1800 he married Barbara Fuhrmann from Danzig. She died on 9 June 1813 in Cape Town, where Ritter also died on 9 September 1810. It is believed that Georg Jacob Ritter, who married Elizabeth Johanna Krynauw on 15 November 1818, was their son. After the Cape became British in 1795, Ritter continued as book-binder in the service of the Government, but nothing came of the plan of the Lords Seventeen to put him in charge of the Government Printing Office as planned during the Dutch régime.

Petrus Borchardus Borcherds, who was born in Cape Town in 1786, wrote *An Auto-biographical Memoir* in 1858 in which he states (p. 172) 'in the year 1799, a printing press had been established, previous to which, and for a hundred and forty-seven years, all laws and proclamations had been written by the pen'. Borcherds unfortunately mentions no printer by name, so it is not known whether he had Harry Harwood Smith or Valentinus Alexius Schoonberg in mind, as it is known that both these printers were active in Cape Town in 1799.

D. H. Varley[2] described a Dutch translation of a letter from the London Missionary Society printed by V. A. Schoonberg in Cape Town in 1799. The eight-page pamphlet, acquired by the South African Public Library in 1946, is a Dutch translation from the English under the title *Brief van het Zendelings Genootschap te London aan de Godsdienst-lievende ingezetenen van de Caap de Goede Hoop;* uit 't Engelsch vertaald en door V. A. Schoonberg gedrukt voor de Zuid-Africaansche Genootschap... 1799. (Letter from the London Missionary Society to the inhabitants of the Cape of Good Hope who love religion; translated from English and printed by V. A. Schoonberg for the South African Society... 1799.) Mr. Varley recorded the fact that the paper bears the watermark 1796, and drew atten-

1. Barnard, Lady Anne. *South Africa a Century ago* ... ed. by W. H. Wilkins. London, Smith, Elder, 1901, p. 305.
2. Varley, D. H. 'An early Cape Printing Discovery' in *Quarterly Bulletin of the South African Library*, vol. 1, No. 1. Sep. 1946, p. 7–12.

tion to the printer's note on the last page of the pamphlet in which he craves the reader's indulgence for having used an occasional 's' instead of a 'z' because of the shortage of type—no doubt an indication of how primitive his printing equipment was.

Valentinus (or Valentyn) Schoonberg (or Schönnberg or Schönberg) was born in Trauenstein in Bavaria in 1749,[1] came to the Cape in 1776, and married Anna Frederica Koning on 8 June 1783, the year in which he obtained burgher rights. He was an educated man and a respected merchant in Cape Town, where he died on 20 May 1825. From the records of the Zuid-Afrikaansche Genootschap it is known that Schoonberg served as Treasurer of the Society, and from the *Transactions* of the London Missionary Society itself[2] it is possible to discover a statement dated 13 May 1799 by the Rev. Dr. J. T. van der Kemp, one of the first missionaries of the Society sent to South Africa, to the effect that 'a Dutch translation of [the Society's] letter is printed on our press'. This statement by Van der Kemp has puzzled everyone, as there is no record of any press at the Cape at this time except the one used by Ritter. It is possible, but unlikely, that Van der Kemp actually brought a press with him when he arrived on 31 March 1799, for it is known that he learned the art of printing before coming to South Africa.[3] It may also be the old Ritter press to which Schoonberg somehow had access, and of which mention is made in the minutes of the Zuid-Afrikaansche Genootschap quoted by Varley[4] to the effect that Schoonberg would pass his press to the Genootschap and that the Society would not need to get one from London. As the Genootschap was a local branch of the London Missionary Society, its press could, no doubt, be described by Van der Kemp as 'our press'.

However this may be, the Schoonberg pamphlet is not only, as Van der Kemp stated, the first South African religious publication, but also the earliest surviving printing item with any pretentions to being a locally printed book, and not an almanac or handbill.

The only other surviving piece of printing produced at the Cape before 1800 is a

1. Moritz, E. *Die deutsche Einwanderung in die niederländische Kapkolonie 1652–1806*. Ludwigsburg, Eichhornverlag, 1943, p. 192.
2. [London] Missionary Society. Transactions [Reprint]. Ann Arbor, University Microfilms, [1965 ?]. vol. 1; 2nd ed. 1795–1802, p. 370.
3. Bruyn, W. van Oosterwijk-. *Dr. Johannes Theodorus van der Kemp, de apostel van Zuid-Afrika, na honderd jaren herdacht, etc.* Utrecht, C. H. E. Breijer, 1896.
4. Varley, D. H., 'An early Cape Printing Discovery' in *Quarterly Bulletin of the South African Library*, vol. 1, No. 1, Sep. 1946, p. 9.

Military Proclamation in English and Dutch, dated 26 February 1799 and signed by Major-General Dundas. It is therefore a little earlier than Schoonberg's work, which could only have been printed after Van der Kemp's arrival, as he brought the original English letter from the London Missionary Society with him.[1]

No printer's name occurs on the military Proclamation of which the Cape Archives has a copy, but it has been generally assumed that Harry Harwood Smith, an English master printer, had a hand in it. The authority for this assumption, no doubt, is the following petition[2] sent by Smith to the Governor Sir George Yonge on 21 April 1800:

The Memorial of Harry Harwood Smith

Sheweth

That having been employed as Clerk and Examiner in the Secretary's Office, from the Month of January 1799, to the present Period—And also assisting to the utmost of his abilities in Printing such Proclamations and Papers as have been required for the Secretary's Office; he humbly requests Your Excellency will be pleased to take the same into consideration—and allow your Memorialist such Salary as Printer to Government that Your Excellency may think just.

And your Memorialist also begs leave to represent, that having received great part of his Printing Materials by the *Dubric*; and expecting the remainder with a Complete Printing Press, in a short time, humbly solicits Your Excellency's Permission, to follow his Profession as Printer, so long as he continues not to interfere in an improper manner with the Religion and Government of the Colony, nor derogatory to the Constitution and Interests of the Mother Country. And for the further information of Your Excellency, your Memorialist begs leave to add, that his intentions are confined merely to Printing such Public Papers, as may be required by the different Departments of Government—Notices & Catalogues of Sales—and things of a similar and mercantile tendency.

It would seem that Smith's petition went unheeded, for on 21 July 1800 Sir George Yonge issued the following proclamation:[3]

Notice is hereby given that Messrs. Walker & Robertson have my permission to set up a printing press and to publish a Newspaper weekly, and the aforesaid persons are to be considered as the Sole printers of Government and the only licensed printers in this Colony; nor shall any Public

1. [London] Missionary Society. Transactions [Reprint]. Ann Arbor, University Microfilms [1965?]. vol. I; 2nd ed. 1795–1802, p. 366.
2. Cape Archives Document BO 32 p. 459–460.
3. Theal, G. M. *Records of the Cape Colony from December 1799 to May 1801*, [London?], printed for the Government of the Cape Colony, 1898 p. 198.

Order, Vendue or Mercantile Notices, Bills of Sale or Advertisements be published but by the said printers, either in their Newspaper, or hand Bills, printed by them, And all matters so printed by them shall be deemed Sufficient Notices of such Matters; and any other person or persons attempting the same will be subject to the prosecution of the Law, besides having their printing Materials Seized and confiscated, and besides paying for every Offence against this Order, on Conviction, a fine of One Thousand Rixdollars.

The effect of this proclamation is clear from the next petition sent by Henry Harwood Smith to the Acting Governor, Major-General Dundas on 4 May 1801:[1]

That I, your Memorialist arrived in this Colony in the Month of January 1799, with a Letter addressed to the Earl of Macartney—recommending me in my profession as Printer; the tenor of which, so far received your Honor's approbation, that I printed during a period of Eighteen Months (as well as the Press in the possession of Government would admit) such Proclamations & other Public Papers as were required; to effect which, in a better manner, an Order for a complete Printing Press and other necessary Materials was given by Mr. Hercules Ross: prior to whose departure for England, my Materials arrived, but unfortunately without a Press; of which circumstance, on informing Mr. Ross, he assured me he would bring a Press on his return; and, by Letters received from England I have reason to believe it has been procured.

On being credibly informed, Messrs. Walker & Robertson intended importing Printers and Materials, to supplant me in my Profession (to acquire which, I faithfully dedicated Seven Years, according to the custom of the City of London; and which Profession I practised as a Master upwards of two Years 'till I left England for the Colony) it became my indispensible duty, to memorial Sir George Yonge on the subject; to which, no favorable Answer was received.

On the 21st of July last, a Proclamation was issued (a copy of which I have the honor to annex) appointing Messrs. Walker and Robertson *sole* Printers to Government; and the only licensed Printers in this Colony, thereby annihilating the hopes I entertained of being continued in the service of Government as Printer; and depriving me of the prospect of maintaining myself and family, by pursuing that profession to which I devoted the early part of my life.

On the 20th of September last, I received orders to deposit my Materials under the care of Government, which I strictly adhered to; the Key of which *Depôt* is in Mr. Barnard's possession.

It is here necessary I should remark for Your Honor's information, that during the period of Eighteen Months, I received *no Salary*, or *other recompense* for Printing beyond what I enjoyed as Clerk in the Secretary's Office, viz. 40 Rix Drs per month.—But, since the deprivation of my Profession, I have received an extra Salary of 50 Rix Drs month.

I have thus intruded on Your Honor's time, the particulars of this Affair, and humbly trust, in consideration of the Character, with which I was first introduced to Your Honor's Notice, (by means of the Letter addressed to the Earl of Macartney) and which character I have hitherto maintained, that Your Honor will be pleased to re-instate me as Printer in the service of Government, with such Salary as the nature of the service may require; And, also, that You will be pleased to grant me permission to follow my Profession, under such restrictions, as Your Honor in your wisdom may think meet.

1. Cape Archives Document BO 32 p. 467–469.

The official reply to this memorial, judging by the endorsement on p. 474 of the document in the Cape Archives merely informed Smith that nothing could be done about the monopoly, and that he was at liberty to lay his claim to be employed as a printer before the new Governor.

In the meantime, from their press situated at their premises at 35 Plein Street, Cape Town, on 16 August 1801, Walker and Robertson issued the first number of South Africa's first serial publication, *The Cape Town Gazette and African Advertiser*, which included both Dutch and English matter. It was published on Saturdays, cost 24 Rixdollars a year, and included proclamations, official notices, some home and foreign news, times of arrival and departure of ships, market prices, notices of auctions and domestic notices.[1] This was the beginnings of the *Government Gazette*, which still exists.

The curious situation, where a firm of general merchants importing, among other commodities, both slaves and books, should be granted a monopoly of printing and have the honour of issuing the first news sheet in South Africa, may be attributed to the fact that the Governor, Sir Geoge Yonge, and Walker and Robertson were apparently associated in questionable commercial dealings, as indicated by R. F. M. Immelman in *Men of Good Hope: the Romantic Story of the Cape Town Chamber of Commerce* (p. 16). The Governor was recalled in April 1801 because of his malpractices, and the firm went bankrupt.

The Government, however, also had misgivings about having placed, what was in effect, an official gazette, in the hands of a private firm, no matter how eminent, as is evident from Acting Governor Major-General Dundas's letter to Lord Hobart, dated 8 October 1801:[2]

I am apt to believe that the disseminating through all the parts of an enlightened Country a general knowledge of public events, through the medium of a Newspaper, is not only gratifying to Individuals but, under proper restrictions, useful in the administration of public affairs. The establishment of a Printing Press nevertheless, during the administration of Sir George Yonge, I conceive to be premature, and more likely to produce evil than good effects, since the minds of the Inhabitants are by no means prepared to exercise the freedom of discussion on almost any subject, particularly politics, concerning which they have been led to entertain very confused and erroneous opinions. The Printing press however having been placed in the hands of private individuals, by the authority of the late Governor, at whose express desire the proprietors were in-

1. Botha, C. G. 'Geskiedenis van die Drukpers in Suid-Afrika' *in Die Huisgenoot*, February 1921, p. 411.
2. Theal, G. M. *Records of the Cape Colony from May 1801 to February 1803*, [London?], printed for the Government of the Cape Colony, 1899 p. 79–82.

duced, at a considerable expence [!], to import the Press from England, I have not thought myself at liberty to deprive them of their privilege of printing, without a proper compensation, and as it was represented to me that the suppression of the press would be attended with many inconveniences to the Merchants and others, I have thought it advisable until honored with Your Lordship's instructions on this subject, the purchasing from the proprietors, on Colonial account, the whole printing apparatus, placing it under the immediate inspection of Government, in the office of the Secretary of the Colony in the Castle, under the superintendency of Mr. Barrow, Auditor of Accounts, who has voluntarily offered his assistance upon this occasion, having perfect confidence in his discretion and judgment in directing the publication of such subjects only as cannot prove injurious to the interests of His Majesty's Government and the public service. The price paid to Messrs. Walker & Robertson, the original proprietors of the Printing Press, for the same, amounts to twelve thousand Rixdollars, equal to Two Thousand Pounds Sterling, which sum the Colonial Treasury will not ultimately lose, there being reasonable ground to hope that, in a very short space of time, the profits arising from Advertisements and Subscriptions for the Paper will fully repay the expense which has been incurred upon this occasion.

The memorial, dated 2 October 1801, from Alexander Walker and John Robertson asking for compensation when the Government took over their printing works has survived in the Cape Archives (Document B O 32), and from it we learn that Robertson spent six months in London obtaining and shipping the equipment—20 tons of it, and that four men were brought from overseas. They were Cornelius Graafland, a translator; George Williams, George Ross, and Edward Smith, all three presumably printers. They arrived at the Cape on 15 June 1800, and started printing on 1 August.

On 10 October 1801 the public was informed by John Barrow, as Superintendent of the Press, that printing work could be done at the Castle at lower rates than those charged by Walker & Robertson.[1] Smith was appointed to the printing office in the Castle after he had once more petitioned the Government,[2] while Ritter continued as book-binder, and judging from the advertisement of 1806 reproduced in Eric Rosenthal's *160 Years of Cape Town Printing*, p. 8, Ritter was working mainly as what is today known as a 'binder and ruler' rather than as an ordinary book-binder.

Under the title of *African Court Calendar for 1801* H. H. Smith was responsible for compiling the first of a long run, under various titles, of 'Cape almanacs' of which the English edition was advertised for publication on 1 December 1801, but of which no

1. Rosenthal, E. *160 Years of Cape Town Printing*. (Cape Town, Cape Town Association of Printing House Craftsmen and the Cape Chamber of Printing, 1960), p. 8.
2. Cape Archives Document BO 32, endorsement on p. 478.

printed copy is known to have survived. There is, however, in the Library of Parliament, Cape Town, a manuscript which may be the original script or a copy made from the printed almanac. The imprint reads 'Cape Town, Printed at the Government Press, 1801'. A Dutch version of the issue for 1801 was advertised to appear on 11 January 1802, but again no copies seem to have survived. Smith compiled almanacs for 1802 and 1803, but no copies of the issue for 1803 are known. Nothing more has been traced about H. H. Smith, except that in March 1803 he announced his intention of leaving the Cape and offered printing materials for sale.[1]

The Rev. Meent Borcherds, who officiated in Stellenbosch from 1786 until 1830, was so pleased because a printing press had been established at the Cape, that he composed a poem in honour of the occasion, which was printed in Cape Town, and acknowledged in the minutes of the meeting of the Society to promote Agriculture, Arts and Science on 1 September 1800.[2] Unfortunately no copy of this, presumably the first, literary product of the Cape press has survived. The same writer was responsible for another poem, *De Maan* (the Moon), of which one copy is preserved in the South African Public Library, Cape Town. Two of the four parts of this poem were published on 24 April 1801,[3] but neither of these literary products sold in sufficient numbers to pay for the paper. Also in 1801, and with the imprint 'Ter drukkery van het Gouvernement No. 35 Plein Straat', was published a religious pamphlet entitled *Troostelyk Gesprek tusschen den Here Jezus en de Moedeloose Ziel* (Comforting Discussion between the Lord Jesus Christ and the Despondent Soul) of which the only known copy was sold to the Kimberley Public Library some thirty years ago by the collector W. R. Morrison. It is obvious that the products of the Cape press before the end of the first British occupation in 1803 are few in number and extremely rare, which is not surprising when one considers how fragile they are. Nothing of any great moment was published, and on the whole the printing is inferior, but they are of great interest as the earliest examples of printing in South Africa.

J. A. de Mist was asked on 4 December 1801 to report on how best to organize matters at the Cape. Within seven weeks he prepared his report which was accepted by the Batavian Government, and De Mist himself was sent to the Cape as Commis-

1. *Government Gazette*, 19 March 1803.
2. Borcherds, M. *De Maan* ... herdrukt naar het oorspronkelijke in 1802 uitgegeven. Kaapstad, Van de Sandt de Villiers, 1857, p. 49.
3. *Cape Town Gazette and African Advertiser*, 24 April 1801.

sioner to implement his recommendations. Item 44 of his Memorandum[1] reads as follows as translated into English:

> ... we feel it incumbent upon ourselves to endorse strongly the recommendations made by the Commissioners-General, to the effect that a *Printing Establishment* should be introduced at Cape Town. There is no denying that it would be of universal benefit to the community. It would ensure the more rapid and efficient, and less expensive circulation of Government proclamations throughout the country districts, where the farmers are scattered hours apart from each other. It would act as a strong incentive to these farmers to learn to read these notices. The misuse of the printing press could be obviated if it were placed under Government supervision. Splendid results would be bound to follow upon the publication in leaflets and in almanacs of simple and well-chosen information on various subjects. In this work the co-operation of a wise Government would be of the utmost importance. The establishment of a printing press would also serve as an antidote against rebellion and ignorance, especially in a country where the aids to moral enlightenment and civilization are so difficult to apply. Under the present English régime, a printing press was immediately erected, and a Cape newspaper is actually published. Such a newspaper, edited by a loyal and efficient individual, could be of incalculable benefit to the Colony. It is impossible to say whether or not this printing press was erected by private enterprise or at the expense of the Government, and we cannot therefore state definitely whether or not the press will still be at the Cape when we take over.

It would seem that the Batavian authorities found a press at the Cape in 1803, and continued to operate a government-controlled printing works, but at least one unauthorized item was issued towards the end of June 1803. This was *Remarques générales sur le Cap de Bonne Espérance* by Baron A. van Pallandt, who was Acting Private Secretary to the Governor, General Janssens, for a time. Fifty copies were printed at the Castle on the Government Press without the knowledge or sanction of the Governor, who was away at the time. De Mist was informed of the publication, which was critical of conditions at the Cape, and he gave orders to search the ship *Spion* before she left for Europe with copies of the booklet. They were confiscated, and the author instructed to destroy a copy in De Mist's presence and to hand over another to him. It is believed that the only known surviving copy in the Cape Archives is the one handed to De Mist. The author was dismissed.

On 7 February 1804 a proclamation was issued by Gen. Janssens concerning security measures and British subjects at the Cape. A copy turned up in the Library of the American Antiquarian Society in Worcester, Massachusetts, and is described by D. McMurtrie in an article, 'The Introduction of Printing into South Africa'

1. Mist, J. A. de. *The Memorandum of Commissary J. A. de Mist* ... with an Eng. version by K. M. Jeffreys, *etc.* Cape Town, Van Riebeeck Society, 1920.

which appeared in *Output*, vol. 2, 1932, No. 7, the house journal of Seligson & Clare.

It is manifestly impossible to note more than a few of the publications emanating from the press in Cape Town even in these early days, so let us see who the printers were who were responsible for the publications.

In the *Lyst van Alle Collegien* (or Cape Almanac) both for 1805 and 1806 a list of officials in the Government Printing Works appears. The Director was Reinier de Klerk Dibbitz; the Master Printer, Andreas Richert; and the three compositors were Willem Dams, Jacobus Andreas Richert and Johannes Richert; together with J. C. Ritter as book-binder, and a book-keeper, a messenger, and three translators.

Reinier de Klerk Dibbitz is an interesting figure, for he was a physician who arrived at the Cape in June 1802 as 'Director-in-Chief of the Great Military Hospital at the Cape of Good Hope' and was closely associated with the introduction to the Cape of vaccination against smallpox.[1] He was born in Batavia on 16 January 1764 and practised as a doctor at Heerenveen in Holland, before coming to the Cape where he combined the posts of chief of the hospital with that of head of the Government Printing Office. He died in April or May 1808 on the coast of Guinea when *en route* for Java from Holland. In 1784 he married Helena Charlotta van Rossum who died at the Cape on 25 April 1805.[2] No information about his knowledge of practical printing has been traced, so possibly he may have been responsible only for administrative duties.

Andreas Richert was born in Berlin on 11 November 1763, arrived at the Cape with his wife and children in 1803, and appears to have been employed in the Government Printing Office at least as early as April 1803. His first wife was Geertruyda Catharina Beukes of The Hague, and his second Sara Maria Bruyns, who died at the Cape on 7 July 1825. There were three sons and a daughter. When the Cape once again became British, after the Battle of Blaauwberg, Andreas Richert was given the option of returning to Europe, but elected to remain in his old post on the same salary as he had had during the Batavian régime.[3] This arrangement was made in February 1806. In 1804 he compiled the *African Court Calendar* and in the same year he was also responsible for printing W. S. van Ryneveld's *Aanmerkingen over de Verbetering van het Vee aan de Kaap de Goede Hoop* (Remarks on the Improve-

1. Burrows, E. H. *A History of Medicine in South Africa up to the End of the Nineteenth Century*. Cape Town, A. A. Balkema, 1958, p. 97.
2. Pama, C. *Die Wapens van die ou Afrikaanse Families, etc.* Kaapstad, A. A. Balkema, 1959, p. 105.
3. Cape Archives Document CO 3856, No. 23.

ment of Cattle at the Cape of Good Hope), a rather more ambitious publication than most of those emanating from the Cape press at that time. The imprint (in translation) reads: 'Printed by A. Richert, book printer of the Government at the Cape of Good Hope' and an imprimatur by the Government Secretary appears on the reverse of the title-page. From internal evidence this work of 104 pages must have been printed between 3 June and 31 Decembei 1804, and at least two copies have survived—one in the S.A. Public Library, Cape Town, and the other in the Johannesburg Public Library.

On various occasions Andreas Richert acted as superintendent of the Government Printing Office, and it is on record that he had 'always evinced an active knowledge in the Practical part of the Printing Art'.[1] On 1 August 1821 he was appointed as Superintendent of the Printing Office, and from 1821 to 1825 his name appears as compiler, vendor, and printer of the Cape almanacs. At this period they are called *African Court Calendar, and Directory*. A sidelight is cast on working conditions of the time by the following letter from Richert to the Governor, Lord Charles Somerset on 3 March 1824:

> I beg leave to represent to you that it is highly necessary, in order to have the Paper neatly printed and regularly forwarded, that the Compositors of this Department attend by turns, during the whole of the Night, previous to the publication every week of the *Cape Town Gazette*, in order to superintend the printing of the same, and to rectify accidents that may occur, to forward the same and count them off to the several Drostdies, and to direct those for the subscribers (about 200) in the Country Districts. And as this requires great attention and punctuality, and is very tiresome and injurious to the Health principally after having been busy the whole day, on account of the encreasing Business, in getting the Paper ready for Press; the Compositors have therefore addressed themselves to me, with request to lay this their case before you, humbly praying, that His Excellency the Governor may be graciously pleased to grant them some remuneration for their Night attendance,...

The Governor sanctioned six Rixdollars for each night.[2]

The troubles of bilingualism were being experienced as early as 1806 when officials in the Printing Office were permitted to translate advertisements for the *Gazette* and to retain any fees. There is a letter extant from Richert dated 23 July 1825 giving information on the distribution of fees so collected, and this unsatisfactory practice was not entirely discontinued until 1829.[3] On 1 August 1825

1. Cape Archives Document CO 141, No. 13.
2. Theal, G. M. *Records of the Cape Colony from June to October 1824*. [London], printed for the Government of the Cape Colony, 1903, p. 200.
3. Cape Archives Documents CO 229 No. 34 and CO 235 No. 73.

Andreas Richert was dismissed, because he had 'been detected in defrauding the Merchants and other Residents of this Town by charging for the insertion of their Advertisements in the *Government Gazette* far beyond what is authorised by the Government Tariff and the extra fees allowed for the Workmen'.[1] Because of this incident, the Government authorities at the Cape protested against the appointment, on 29 May 1827, of Richert as Consul at the Cape to the King of Prussia. The *Gazette* of 4 June 1830 noted Andreas Richert's death in Cape Town on 22 May 1830 at the age of 66 years 6 months and 11 days.

Of the three compositors listed as employed in the Government Printing Office in 1805 and 1806 two were sons of Andreas Richert. The elder of the two was Jacobus Andreas, born at The Hague in 1789, and employed as an apprentice in the Government Printing Office from 1 April 1803. He died on 3 July 1815, at the age of nearly twenty-six years according to the notice inserted in the *Government Gazette* of 8 July 1815 by his widow.

Johannes Richert also came to the Cape with his father Andreas Richert in 1803, having been born in Holland in 1791. He presumably started his apprenticeship in the Government Printing Office on 1 June 1804 and completed it by 9 January 1812, earning the praise of his superiors.[2] By 1 August 1821 he had been appointed printer in the Dutch Department at an annual salary of £100.[3] In the Almanac of 1827 his name appears at the head of the 'Dutch Department', but after this year, his name no longer appears, and the assumption is that he was working for an independent firm of printers.

By the middle 'thirties he was a partner in the firm of Richert, Pike & Co., and died on 14 October 1843 in Cape Town, leaving a widow, Anna Carolina Langermann.

The last of the compositors listed as being in the Government Printing Office in 1805 and 1806 is the senior man, Willem Dams. All that is known of him is that he was born in 'Hertogenbos' and died on 3 November 1809 at the age of just over thirty-eight years.[4]

Except for the appointment of George Ross as Superintendent in place of De Klerk Dibbitz, the staff of the Government Printing Office remained the same in

1. Theal, G. M. *Records of the Cape Colony from February to June 1827*. [London], printed for the Government of the Cape Colony, 1905, p. 415.
2. Cape Archives Document CO 37, No. 12.
3. Theal, G. M. *Records of the Cape Colony from December 1827 to April 1831*. [London?], printed for the Government of the Cape Colony, 1905, p. 46.
4. *Government Gazette*, 4 November 1809.

1807 and 1808 as it had been during the Batavian period. Little is known of George Ross, who was brought out by Walker & Robertson in 1800, presumably from London, and signed the oath of allegiance to the Batavian Government on 21 November 1803.[1] His name appears on the title-pages of the *Cape Almanacs* as compiler and printer at the Government Printing Office from 1807 to 1820, except for 1814, when he was on leave overseas and Andreas Richert acted for him. He was again on leave in 1820.[2] There is a letter of his from London dated 20 April 1821 to the Cape authorities explaining that as he could not obtain permission to extend his leave beyond 31 December 1820, and as he was forced by family affairs to overstay his leave, he had no alternative but to resign. In official correspondence dated 7 August 1825, relating to the payment of fees for translating advertisements into Dutch, mention is made of 'the late Mr. Ross'.[3] The assumption is therefore that he died between April 1821 and August 1825, but whether at the Cape or overseas is not known.

In 1809 Bernardus Josephus van de Sandt makes his appearance as an apprentice in the Printing Office. George Ross, in writing to the Colonial Secretary on 29 November 1809, noted that Van de Sandt was the step-son of the late compositor Willem Dams.[4] It is believed that his father was Barend van de Sandt from the Dutch province of Gelderland who died at the Cape on 28 November 1804 at the age of thirty-five. In giving evidence on 4 June 1824, Bernardus Josephus van de Sandt stated that he was twenty-five years of age and had been born at the Cape.[5] His birthplace is thought to have been the Paarl, and he is therefore the first South African to be trained as a printer. He became Superintendent of the Printing Office in 1832, and held this position until the Office was closed down in 1844.[6] In the Cape Archives is a letter from Van de Sandt to John Montagu, Secretary to the Government, dated 5 February 1845, in which an account is enclosed of the auction sale of the printing materials which had belonged to the Government. Van de

1. Cape Archives Document BR 119, p. 119.
2. *Government Gazette*, 22 April 1820.
3. Theal, G. M. *Records of the Cape Colony from June to August 1825*. [London?] printed for the Government of the Cape Colony, 1904, p. 452.
4. Cape Archives Document CO 14 No. 53.
5. Theal, G. M. *Records of the Cape Colony from June to October 1824*. [London], printed for the Government of the Cape Colony, 1903, p. 85.
6. Bosman, F. C. L. 'Uit die Geskiedenis van Almanakke in Suid-Afrika' in *Jaarboek van die Nederduits-Gereformeerde Kerke in Suid-Afrika, 1931*, p. 79.

Sandt reported that the prices had been lower than he had expected, and that he had bought some of the items himself. He also noted that some of the material had been in use for more than thirty years.[1] Van de Sandt in later years played an important part in printing almanacs (from 1836 to 1850), some important newspapers, and numerous books. He died in Cape Town in January 1850.

By the time the *Cape Almanac* for 1820 was in preparation, three new names appear among those in the Printing Office—W. S. Bridekirk, Jr., A. Richert, Jr., and T. Hammond.

L. H. Meurant, who was in the position to know, states that William Storey Bridekirk was a nephew of the Port Captain William Bridekirk.[2] He was born in South Shields, County Durham, the son of William Bridekirk and his wife Mary Storey,[3] arrived in Table Bay on 30 July 1817, and, as a trained printer, immediately applied for a post as compositor in the Printing Office.[4] On 4 August 1824 he resigned in order to establish a printing works on his own account.[5] He died on 8 September 1843 in Cape Town at the age of forty-seven and left a widow, Eliza Griffith.

Perhaps because of the part Bridekirk played in the struggle for the freedom of the press, he has not always received the credit due to him as a printer. His work certainly was not inferior to that of any of his contemporaries, and he was responsible for a variety of important publications. Among these Suasso de Lima's *Geschiedenis van de Kaap de Goede Hoop* (1825) should be noted as the first history of the Cape. It is in the form of question and answer. The number of shipwrecks in South African waters is legion, and it is of interest to see that Bridekirk was responsible for printing the French account *Relation du Naufrage du Navire français l'Eole* (1829). Various periodicals were printed by him, such as some issues of *The Colonist* (1827), and *The Cape of Good Hope Literary Gazette* (1830–1834). *The Report of the Society for the Relief of Distressed Settlers* (1824) must be one of his earliest publications after leaving the Government Printing Office.

Andreas Richert, Jr., was the youngest son of Andreas Richert (1763–1830) and was born at The Hague in 1799. On the request of his father, the son was apprenticed as a compositor in the Printing Office on 10 February 1813,[6] and remained there at least until 23 August 1825. His death occurred in Cape Town on 5 June 1829.

1. Cape Archives Document CO 4027 No. 560, p. 1–2. 2. Meurant, L. H. *Sixty Years ago; or, Reminiscences of the Struggle for the Freedom of the Press in South Africa, etc.* Cape Town, Saul Solomon, 1885, p. 74. 3. Death notice 6337 in the Cape Archives. 4. Cape Archives Document CO 80 No. 80. 5. Cape Archives Document CO 207 No. 33. 6. Cape Archives Document CO 90 No. 68.

Thomas Hammond, William Bridekirk, and B. J. van de Sandt were involved in printing the proclamation offering a reward in connexion with the posting of a placard libelling the Governor, Lord Charles Somerset, and Dr. James Barry. When Hammond was questioned under oath on 11 June 1824 in connexion with this matter, he stated that he was 'of competent age' and had been employed in the Government Printing Office between five and six years and that he was a compositor.[1] The only other information traced is to be found in the following notice in *The South African Chronicle* of 5 July 1825, which reads that Thomas Hammond, compositor in the Government Printing Office 'in a fit of insanity put a period to his existence yesterday morning near the premises of the late Major Zorn'.

On 14 April 1820, Sir Rufane Donkin, Acting Governor of the Cape of Good Hope requisitioned the following printing materials for the Government Printing office:[2]

2000 lbs. Long Primer, No. 6, with a proportion of Signs, Superiors, 2 line Letters, open Letters, half fractions, space Rules, and a double proportion of the Letters, d, k, n, r, v, y, and z.
1000 lbs. Brevier, No. 4, with a proportion as above.
500 lbs. English, No. 7, as above.
500 lbs. Double Pica, No. 3, as above.
500 lbs. Great Primer, No. 3, as above.
500 lbs. Two line English, No. 3, as above.
2 Stanhope Presses with everything complete.
3000 Ball Nails.
6 Brass Column Galleys.
12 Mallets.
12 Mahogany Plainers.
150 Shooting Sticks.
10 dozen foot and side Sticks.
12 pr. Letter Cases.
1 cask Pot Ash (fine American).

This order had an interesting sequel. On 16 October 1820 George Ross wrote from London to inform Lord Charles Somerset, the Governor, 'that Mr. Clowes, the Printer, who furnishes the materials' was of the opinion of 'the necesity of employing and sending out with the Stanhope Presses a person capable of superintending them,

1. Theal, G. M. *Records of the Cape Colony from June to October 1824*. [London ?], printed for the Government of the Cape Colony, 1903, p. 102.
2. Theal, G. M. *Records of the Cape Colony from January 1820 to June 1821*. [London ?], printed for the Government of the Cape Colony, 1902, p. 175.

both as to the erecting of them, and preserving them in their perfect state of repair'.[1] The man selected to take charge was Jesse Marsh, who was given financial assistance with his passage money,[2] and given an advance of £30 to be deducted when he was employed in the Government Printing Office at the Cape.[3] He arrived together with his wife, from Portsmouth, on 24 May 1821.[4]

On 8 January 1824 the Superintendent of the Printing Office reported Marsh for continual drunkenness and neglect of duty. It was stated that he had absented himself for nearly three weeks and that he intended to engage himself to George Greig, the only independent printer in Cape Town. His dismissal was authorized[5] but as the post of pressman could not be filled, it was necessary to use slave labour for a time and to run the risk of damage to the presses.[6]

From a memorial by Marsh dated 25 July 1825 to the Secretary to the Cape Government, it is learnt that Marsh had also worked for Bridekirk.[7] From another memorial of his dated 30 April 1827, it is clear that he 'had a thorough knowledge of both branches [compositor and pressman, presumably] in the art of Printing for the last 27 years' (excepting 5 years in His Majesty's Service) and that he would like to work for Greig if Greig 'is allowed to continue his Paper.'[8] Marsh was in receipt of a naval pension.[9] It is not known whether he returned to England or stayed at the Cape.

The name of Peter McDougal appears for the first time in the *Cape Almanac* of 1823 as a mem ber of the staff of the Printing Office, and heis still to be found as a compositor in the issue for 1854. Otherwise nothing is known about him.

Louis Henri Meurant in *Sixty Years ago*[10] notes that there were four practical printers, as he calls them, among the British Settlers who came to South Africa in 1820. They were R. Godlonton, William Cock, Thomas Stringfellow, and Samuel Mollett. Godlonton and Stringfellow played an important part in the development

1. *Ibidem*, p. 301.
2. *Ibidem*, p. 360.
3. Cape Archives Document GH 1/6 No. 336.
4. *Government Gazette*, 26 May 1821.
5. Cape Archives Document CO 207 No. 4.
6. Robinson, A. M. Lewin. *None daring to make us afraid, etc.* Cape Town, Maskew Miller, 1962, p. 20.
7. Cape Archives Document CO 235 No. 115.
8. Cape Archives Document CO 3933 No. 246, p. 1–2.
9. Theal, G. M. *Records of the Cape Colony from August 1822 to May 1823, etc.* [London?], printed for the Government of the Cape Colony, 1903, p. 132.
10. Meurant, L. H. *Sixty Years ago; or, Reminiscences of the Struggle for the Freedom of the Press in South Africa, etc.* Cape Town, Saul Solomon, 1885, p. 8.

of printing in Grahamstown, while William Cock from Oxfordshire seems not to have practised his craft in South Africa. Samuel Mollett, who died in Cape Town on 30 April 1840 aged seventy-two years and four months,[1] came out on the *Nautilus* as a member of Crause's party. On 25 August 1825 Bridekirk stated that Mollett was employed by him, and Meurant records Mollett as having become 'overseer in the printing office of Mr. W. Bridekirk, proprietor of the *South African Chronicle*, Cape Town'. He is recorded as printing the *Cape Town Gazette and African Advertiser* (in other words the Government Gazette) 'for the contractor' from 3 July 1835 until his death, some English publications, including a pamphlet on Dr. Andrew Smith's expedition to the interior issued in 1836, and various Dutch works, including a pamphlet of thirty-five pages with illustrations entitled *Levens Geschiedenis van Mevrouw Paterson* (The life story of Mrs. Paterson) in 1837. Between 7 and 9 July 1824 Mollett was nominated by Lord Charles Somerset together with a Mr. Johnstone to value George Greig's printing materials when they were surrendered to the Government. It is interesting to note that the list has survived and covers ten foolscap pages. The valuation amounted to £848.13.11¾. according to documents enclosed with Lord Charles Somerset's letter to Earl Bathurst on 12 March 1825[2] concerning the struggle for the freedom of the press at the Cape.

The names W. R., R., and J. Johnstone occur in the records, and it is believed that they refer to different men, who worked in the Government Printing Office. A list, concerning increases in the salaries of Cape civil servants made during the quarter ending 30 June 1826, records that W. R. Johnstone was a compositor in the Printing Office, whose salary had been raised on 11 April from £75 to £100 per annum and continues, 'on a vacancy occurring among the compositors of the printing office in June 1825, it was deemed necessary to procure a competent person regularly brought up to the business from England, and £100 a year was authorized to be held out as a salary to such a person who would contract with the Government for three years. Mr. Johnstone arrived in consequence'.[3] As these are the words of Major-General R. Bourke, the Lieutenant-Governor, writing to Earl Bathurst, the Secretary of State for the Colonies, the date may have been misread by Theal in transcribing and should be June 1823, or, of course, W.R. may not be the man who did the valuation in 1824.

1. *Cape of Good Hope Eastern Districts Government Gazette*, 14 May 1840.
2. Theal, G. M. *Records of the Cape Colony from February to April 1825, etc.* [London?], printed for the Government of the Cape Colony, 1904, p. 146–151.
3. Theal, G. M. *Records of the Cape Colony from June to September 1826, etc.* [London?], printed for the Government of the Cape Colony, 1905, p. 311–312.

This completes the list of printers at work in Cape Town from the time of Ritter to the arrival of George Greig on 9 March 1823 and the establishment of his printing works on 8 September of the same year.[1] The desire for another printing press besides that in possession of the Government was expressed on various occasions, notably by William Dunn on 9 June 1821, when he pleaded for a weekly journal in which information on agricultural matters could be provided.[2] W. W. Bird in his *State of the Cape in 1822* had much to say on the state of reading and in particular on the Printing Office which he calls 'a degraded establishment'. He records that it annually prints a Cape calendar and almanac, and a weekly newspaper called the *Cape Gazette*, which contains nothing but a list of proclamations; civil and military appointments and promotions; marriages and other personal notices; the price of produce; advertisements of sales; and official notices. No European news, no parliamentary debates, nothing scientific—in fact nothing of real interest was in his view to be found in the *Gazette*. For the rest, the press, according to Bird, was occupied in printing handbills and notices.[3] A similar picture of the intellectual life at the Cape is given by the anonymous author of *Notes on the Cape of Good Hope, made during an Excursion in that Colony in the Year 1820:*

> Literature is wholly neglected. The chaplain of the garrison takes in a few pupils; but there is no school in the colony. A good schoolmaster is much wanted. Such as can afford it, among the English, give their children an education at home. The Dutch go without.
>
> A fine collection of the Latin and Greek classics was left to the public, by an old German gentleman, who died here; and they are deposited in a room adjoining to the Lutheran church, called the *Public Library*. However, a friend of mine applying for admission, it was thought to be an innovation upon established rules, and so hazardous a step, that the colonial secretary was consulted upon the occasion!
>
> There is a subscription reading-room, whose shelves are supplied with a very few novels, and books of travels; and one circulating library, to which Tom Jones and Humphrey Clinker have not yet found their way. Intellectual refinement is, in fact, at the lowest ebb, both among the Dutch and English.[4]

In July 1823 John Thomas Bigge, William M. G. Colebrooke, and W. Blair arrived. They were sent to the Cape by the Imperial Government as Commissioners to

1. Robinson, A. M. Lewin. *None daring to make us afraid, etc.* Cape Town, Maskew Miller, 1962, p. 20 and 22.
2. Theal, G. M. *Records of the Cape Colony from June 1821 to August 1822*, etc. [London?], printed for the Government of the Cape Colony, 1902, p. 22.
3. Bird, W. W. *State of the Cape in 1822.* London, 1823, p. 58–59.
4. *Notes of the Cape of Good Hope, made during an Excursion in that Colony in the Year 1820.* London, John Murray, 1821, p. 103.

investigate the administration and finances of the Colony, and in their report[1] dated 6 September 1826, to Earl Bathurst reviewed the printing position and reported as follows:

A revenue has been nominally derived by the colonial government from the profits of a printing establishment maintained at the public expense. It existed under the Batavian government, and continued until the year 1824 to engross the whole of the printing business of the colony, either for the government or for individuals. Certain fees having been improperly taken and appropriated by the superintendent to himself and others in the printing office, the department was regulated in the last year, and a new superintendent appointed.

Since the establishment of two private presses in Cape Town, much of the business formerly performed in the government printing office has been withdrawn from it; and although it continues to print for the public, and has the benefit of advertisements, the charges for which are regulated by tariff, the profits arising from this source have been much reduced.

On the other hand, it has been found expedient to limit the government gazette printed at this office to the publication of the ordinances and regulations of the government, and to such private advertisements as are offered.

The department has been lately engaged in printing a compilation of the laws and regulations of the colony in English and Dutch, from the year 1806 to the present time; and it is ordinarily employed in printing the various blank returns and papers required by the public departments.

Considering that the annual expenses of this department are 1,735 L. sterling, and that it is expedient that the government should relinquish the profit it derives from private business, which for the most part is now performed by two private presses, we are of opinion that the estimated profit of 838 l. per annum would not be an object for which the maintenance of such an establishment would be justified, admitting that the department was a source of real profit to this extent. We are therefore of opinion, that the government printing office may be advantageously reduced; and that the printing business of the government, including the publication of ordinances and government advertisements, may be contracted for by a private printer. But as occasions may arise which require extraordinary dispatch and secrecy, it will be expedient to employ a small printing press in one of the government offices, the expense of which will be very inconsiderable.

We cannot doubt that the printing business of the government would be an object of considerable importance to a printer, who would undertake it upon terms more advantageous to the public, than are comprehended in the permanent and contingent charges of a stipendiary department.

The 'two private presses' mentioned by the Commissioners as being in existence in 1826 must have been those of George Greig and William Storey Bridekirk. How

1. Great Britain. *Cape of Good Hope: reports of the Commissioners of Inquiry 1. Upon the administration of the Government at the Cape of Good Hope: 2. Upon the finance at the Cape of Good Hope.* 1827 (282), p. 58–59 *or* in Theal, G. M. *Records of the Cape Colony from June to September 1826, etc.* [London?], printed for the Government of the Cape Colony, 1905, p. 453–454.

it came about that two independent presses were established at this time is part of the story of the struggle for the freedom of the press in South Africa, and here George Greig played a leading part.

Very little seems to be known of George Greig. He was born in 1799,[1] presumably in London, where it is believed he died before 1875. Greig himself stated that he was by profession a printer and had been on the establishment of His Majesty's printing office in London[2] before coming to the Cape. His brother, William, resided in London, and upon occasion was involved in the negotiations between George Greig and the Imperial Government. George Greig was married, but his wife's name has not been found, and it is not known how many children they had.

Shortly after he arrived at the Cape on 9 March 1823 from Portsmouth with some printing materials, George Greig announced in the *Gazette* of 23 August 1823, from 1 Longmarket Street, that he intended to start as a jobbing printer in September. L. H. Meurant remembered how almost at the same time a vessel arrived in Table Bay on her way to India, having on board a quantity of new printing type destined for a periodical in India. As this publication had unexpectedly ceased, efforts were made to sell the type in Cape Town. Meurant's father purchased the type for £300 for Greig on condition that his only son, Louis Henri Meurant, should be taught the art of printing, and, when old enough, be taken in the business as a partner.[3]

Greig added to his plant by the loan of 'two presses, with one small Bellows Press, with types, etc.' from Dr. John Philip of the London Missionary Society.[4] One of the presses, according to Dr. Philip, had been brought to the Cape before 1814, the year Lord Charles Somerset became Governor, and the other in 1819.[5] These presses were used by Greig to print South Africa's first newspaper, *The South African Commercial Advertiser*, of which the first issue appeared on 7 January 1824. They were impounded by the Cape Government when Greig's plant was confiscated. There was endless correspondence between Dr. Philip, the Cape Governor,

1. Pringle, Thomas. *Narrative of a Residence in South Africa;* with intro., biographical and historical notes by A. M. Lewin Robinson, *etc.* Cape Town, C. Struik, 1966, p. 343.
2. Great Britain. *Cape of Good Hope (South African Commercial Advertiser)* ... papers relating to the *South African Commercial Advertiser*, and its Editor Mr. George Greig. 1827. Command Paper No. 470, p. 4.
3. Meurant, L. H. *Sixty Years ago, etc.* Cape Town, Saul Solomon, 1885, p. 13.
4. Theal, G. M. *Records of the Cape Colony from June to October 1824, etc.* [London?], printed for the Government of the Cape Colony, 1903, p. 347.
5. *Ibidem*, p. 353.

and the Imperial Authorities in consequence before the matter was finally cleared up.

The full story of the fight for the freedom of the press at this time has been told by Thomas Pringle in his *Narrative of a Residence in South Africa*,[1] as he saw it from the editorial side of the *South African Commercial Advertiser*, for after the second issue of this weekly, Greig enlisted the help of both Thomas Pringle and John Fairbairn 'to undertake the literary management of the paper'. From the point of view of a practising printer the story has been told by one of George Greig's three compositors at the time, L. H. Meurant, in *Sixty Years Ago*.[2]

Although the Governor, Lord Charles Somerset, was conscious of the danger he saw in a free press, he allowed Greig's paper to run for seventeen issues without undue interference, but when court cases began to be reported, he felt it necessary to intervene, and called for proofs before the eighteenth issue of 5 May 1824 was published. To Greig, Fairbairn, and Pringle this was censorship in the extreme, which they refused to tolerate. So after having submitted their proofs, which received the official imprimatur, they added the following 'Postscript'.[3]

POSTSCRIPT.

Wednesday Morning, One o'clock.

His Majesty's Fiscal having assumed the Censorship of the *South African Commercial Advertiser* by an Official Order, sent to the printing office by a messenger late in the evening before publication, demanding *proof sheets* of the paper for next day [this day] and prohibiting its being struck off 'till we had received his further instructions thereon,' we find it our duty, as BRITISH SUBJECTS, under these circumstances, to discontinue the publication of the said paper, *for the present*, in this Colony, until we have applied for redress and direction to His Excellency, the Governor and the British Government.

Our numerous subscribers will, we trust, require no further explanation at present of this distressing interruption. They, and the rest of the world, shall be speedily put in possession of a full statement of all the Facts:—one of which is a demand from the Fiscal of Two Securities, on or before Friday next, to become bound, under a penalty of TEN THOUSAND RIXDOLLARS [£750] that nothing *offensive* shall appear in any future number—such as extracts from the experienced work of the Civil Servant, a work published in this Colony, this year, by W. W. Bird, Esq., *Comptroller of Customs, and Assessor of the Court of Appeals.*

1. Pringle, T. *African Sketches.* London, Edward Moxon, 1834. Pt. 2: 'Narrative of a Residence in South Africa'.
2. Meurant, L. H. *Sixty Years ago; or, Reminiscences of the Struggle for the Freedom of the Press in South Africa, etc.* Cape Town, Saul Solomon, 1885.
3. *Ibidem*, p. 52.

We will only mention further, at present, that not a word of this our last number has been written, or *altered*, in consequence of the abovementioned transactions, excepting this notice.

Greig's next move was to send two advertisements concerning the stopping of the *South African Advertiser* to the *Government Gazette*. They were both refused. So, the one announcing the publication of 'Facts connected with the Stopping of the Press, and the Censorship of the Fiscal' was printed as a hand-bill, and posted outside. These placards were promptly removed on the instructions of the Fiscal, an official combining the functions of an Attorney-General and a Chief of Police. Work, nevertheless, continued on the composing of the promised statement of the facts, so that the type would be standing ready for printing on the following Monday morning. On the Sunday afternoon, however, officials entered Greig's premises with a warrant 'to seal up all and every *press*, or *presses*, of him the said George Greig, in order to remain so sealed up until His Majesty's pleasure shall be known'. George Greig was at the same time directed to leave the Colony within one month.

The bar-handle of the press was fastened to the cheek with red tape and a seal, and the officials left thinking they had prevented the publication of the 'Facts'. To the matter standing in type, the warrant, and an account of the day's happenings were added, and by working all night, it was possible to distribute the leaflets free to the people of Cape Town on the Monday morning. Although they had no press, Greig's staff managed by using a press-blanket and mallet and planer to produce the required impressions. Understandably, these leaflets are today extremely rare, but a few do exist in , for instance, the libraries of Cape Town and Johannesburg.

Greig duly left for England, obtained authority to continue publishing the *South African Commercial Advertiser* on certain conditions, and publication was resumed on 31 August 1824, with John Fairbairn as editor.

Pringle and Meurant were both interested parties and saw Lord Charles Somerset as nothing but a tyrant and despotic ruler as far as the freedom of the press was concerned, while the Governor in his despatches and Greig in his memorials saw only their respective sides of the problem. The most dispassionate account by contemporaries is to be found in the Report of the Commissioners of Enquiry to Earl Bathurst, under the heading 'Criminal Law and Jurisprudence: Press'. On 18 August 1827 they wrote as follows from Mauritius:[1]

1. Theal, G. M. *Records of the Cape Colony from August to October 1827, etc.* [London?], printed for the Government of the Cape Colony, 1905, p. 21–28.

It would appear from a reference to the records of the Dutch Government that very strong objections were made by the Directors of the Dutch East India Company to the introduction and use of the Press at the Cape, and that upon an application of the inhabitants for leave to import one for the sole purpose of securing a more correct knowledge of the various laws which were transmitted for their observance, the Directors replied that such an object would be as easily accomplished by causing printed copies of the Laws to be transmitted from Holland to the Colony. The restraints, therefore, to which the Press in Holland had been made subject both by Placaats of the States General and by resolutions of the High Courts and until a recent period by the licenses of the Municipal Corporations, did not become necessary, altho' there is abundant reason to presume that the introduction of a Press into the Colony by an Individual would have been accompanied by the most severe conditions and restrictions.

It was not until the year 1800 that a Printing Press imported by two Individuals was allowed to be established by the authority of Governor Sir George Yonge, who publicly notified his permission to them to print a weekly newspaper, and declared them to be the only licensed printers in the Colony, with a threat of prosecution against any other person who should set up a press, of confiscation thereof and of the printing materials, together with a fine of 1,000 Rixdollars.

The Local Government being desirous of obtaining complete control over this Press, contracted with the proprietors for the purchase of it, and an individual of high authority under the Government was appointed to conduct it with the title of 'Superintendant of the Press'.

The office and establishment was remodelled by the Batavian Commissioner in 1803 under the superintendance of an individual who was appointed from Holland and received a salary from Government, to whom all profits derived from advertisements and sale were accounted for or paid.

The conduct of the Press then became subject to the control of the Procurator General, to whom the proof sheets were submitted for 'Fiat', and nothing was to be inserted by Individuals, or even by the Civil Servants, which had not been sanctioned by the Governor.

The Government Press thus continued to possess the exclusive right of printing in the Colony, and the application of an Englishman to introduce another and to print a newspaper in the Dutch and English languages was refused.

After the occupation of the Colony by the British Forces in 1806 little alteration took place in the conduct of the Government Printing Establishment, except by the appointment of an Editor by the Local Government in the year 1822, whose duties appear to have been limited to the selection of articles from English or Foreign Newspapers for insertion in the Government *Gazette*.

During the whole of this period and until the establishment of a Press and the publication of a journal called the *South African Commercial Advertiser* on the 7th January 1824, the Government Press enjoyed the exclusive right of printing for the Public and of publishing a weekly gazette, one of the Missionary Societies being only permitted to print hymns and tracts for the use of its congregation at a Private Press. Other attempts had been made to introduce Presses and to commence the publication of Periodical works for the instruction of the Colony, but they had been uniformly discouraged or resisted, while no exertion was made by the Government to give a more agreeable or instructive form to the only journal which it sanctioned, or to restore to it the character of utility and intelligence which it once possessed under the direction of its first superintendent.

This circumstance and the arrival of the English Emigrants in the year 1820 led to the application which was transmitted to your Lordship, and which was followed by your permission for the publication of a Periodical work entitled the *South African Magazine*, with an understanding, which was verbally communicated to the Parties, that all Controversial Points in religion and politics were to be avoided.

The official interference of His Majesty's Fiscal, and a caution which he deemed it expedient to give to the editor of this journal in consequence of some animadversions which appeared in the 2nd number upon the policy and measures of the Colonial Government in the settlement of the English Emigrants, and which was followed by an Interview between the Governor and the Editor, upon which we were instructed to make a special Report to your Lordship, induced the Editor and another person who had joined him to discontinue their journal. Nearly at the same period measures were taken by the Fiscal for controlling and afterwards for suspending the use of a Press which had been established by an Individual at Cape Town for the general business of Printing and for the publication of a weekly Journal entitled *The South African Commercial Advertiser.*

This measure of precautionary interference, as well as that of which we have just made mention, was founded upon the instructions to the Court of Justice and the Procurator General, which were framed by the Batavian Commissioner in 1804 and which the Fiscal considered to be applicable to any attempt (whether made verbally or in a written or printed publication) to bring the Government or its measures into contempt. The Fiscal also considered that the Editor of the Weekly Journal had transgressed the terms of a prospectus which he had published on the 20th December 1823, in which it was declared that 'the *South African Commercial Advertiser* would most rigidly exclude all personal controversy however disguised or the remotest discussion of subjects relating to the Policy or administration of the Colonial Government'. For although the sanction of the Governor to an application made by this individual in July 1823 for establishing a Press, and for printing a Literary and Commercial Magazine, had been declined upon the ground of preference due to other and earlier applicants in the event of a Press being established in the Colony, and although a later application for the Governor's patronage to the publication of the *South African Commercial Advertiser*, enclosing the prospectus dated 20th December 1823, had remained unanswered and unnoticed, yet the Fiscal considered that document as having pledged the Printer to a course which as long as it was observed might remain unobstructed and required no interference from him as guardian of the public tranquillity. The Press and the Public Journal were thus established and continued for the space of four months under a tacit and implied consent of the Colonial Government, and the suspension of them was effected by a warrant of the Governor addressed to His Majesty's Fiscal, and which was executed by a Judicial Commission authorized by the Chief Justice. It also contained an order to the individual (which was afterwards withdrawn) to leave the Colony 'on account of personal conduct' alleged to be 'subversive of due submission to the lawful commands of the constituted authorities'.

In consequence of an attempt that was made to publish certain anonymous statements reflecting upon the measures adopted by the Fiscal in the suspension of the Press, a proclamation dated 11th June 1824 was issued, by which it was required that every person who should in future print any book or paper meant to be published and dispersed should print also his name and place of abode under a penalty of two hundred rixdollars, with liability to punishment by the Colonial Law if the contents should be criminal. It was not intended however that this law should alter or modify the prohibition to print or publish without license, which had been declared by the proclamation of Sir George Yonge.

After the suspension of the *Commercial Advertiser*, a notice was published in the *Government Gazette* that any persons competent to undertake the publication of a Periodical English Miscellany upon the terms proposed by the Editor of the *South African Magazine*, or a weekly paper upon the terms proposed by the Printer of the *South African Commercial Advertiser* on 20th December 1823, should address themselves to the Assistant Colonial Secretary, and that the Editor of the Magazine should be allowed the use of the Government Press, and should receive every encouragement.

Permission was given by the Governor to two Individuals to establish a Printing Press and to publish a newspaper entitled the *South African Chronicle and Mercantile Advertiser* upon a pledge which was given of their personal securities 'for the strict exclusion of political or personal controversy'.

A sum of money was also advanced by the Lombard Bank (in consequence of a communication from the Colonial Government to the President and Directors) upon the security of the printing materials to enable the individual who had purchased them to commence his business.

We do not think it necessary here to recapitulate the representations that were addressed to your Lordship in England by the individual whose press had been suspended, and whose journal had been to a certain degree superseded by the arrangement to which we have just adverted, and we will briefly allude to the proceedings of the Governor and Lieutenant Governor in Council relative to the Press, as constituting what under your Lordship's instructions must be taken to be the present rule for the guidance and control of publishers of journals or periodical works.

Under the arrangement made with the individual whose Press had been suspended, he received on his return to the Colony a license to resume the publication of the *South African Commercial Advertiser*, after signing and subscribing the conditions contained in his prospectus of the 20th December 1823, and it was understood that the Governor and Council were to have the power of determining how far he adhered to it, and (after a caution once given) of suspending the publication, but that such decision would rest upon their responsibility, which would equally include a suspension, in consequence of his discussing Colonial measures with intemperance or personality in the fair spirit of those expressions, and a discussion of subjects which on account of their peculiar local importance might in the judgment of the Governor and Council endanger the peace and safety of the Colony. A suspension of the Journal was not however necessarily to imply the suspension of his Press, if used for other and general purposes of printing.

With regard to all other periodical works, it is now understood that a License is necessary to legalise the publication of them at the Cape, that a discretion which is to be regulated by a consideration of the circumstances of each case is vested in the Governor and Council of granting or withholding a license, and that none is to be granted unless the applicant shall consent to furnish a previous exposition of the character of his intended publication, by which he is afterwards to be guided, but that the adherence to restrictions upon future discussion is not required to be so strict as that which had been voluntarily proposed in the prospectus of 20th December 1823.

Under these instructions the Governor and Lieutenant Governor in Council have given notice to four individuals who had published Periodical works without previous licenses, to make applications for them, that the future publication of them without license would be illegal, and in consequence of a transgression of the terms of his prospectus by the Publisher of the *South African Commercial Advertiser* and the commencement of a second Journal without a license, the Lieutenant Governor in Council proceeded to admonish him of the necessity of conforming himself to them and of obtaining a license.

We are not aware that a similar caution was given to him by His Majesty's Fiscal, and no criminal prosecution was instituted, but we understood that the Fiscal would not have considered himself precluded from adopting such a course by the instructions and authority which had been transmitted to the Governor in Council, if even he had been made officially acquainted with them.

We do not advert to the later instruction of your Lordship by which the publication of the *South African Commercial Advertiser* has been again suspended, nor to the reasons assigned for it, because we understood that the measure had originated in representations made to your Lordship in England, and we do not find that the insertion of the observations entitled 'Mr. Buissinne's case' in the paper of the 24th May 1826 was specially referred to by the Lieutenant Governor and Council in the admonition which was given to the Printer on the 4th August of the same year, although they stated generally that he had in many instances greatly transgressed the most liberal interpretation of the terms of his prospectus, a fact of which we think that no doubt can be entertained.

Your Lordship is in possession of two Petitions, one of which was addressed to His Majesty in Council in December 1824, praying for the removal of all restrictions upon the freedom of the Press, and signed by 209 individuals, of whom 157 are English, comprising chiefly those of the mercantile class at Cape Town, and several of the emigrant settlers in the District of Albany, and the remainder were Dutch, but comprising a smaller proportion distinguished by wealth or respectability. The second Petition was addressed to the House of Commons, and amongst other things prayed for the liberty of the Press duly established by Law.

We believe that this feeling is now generally entertained in the Colony, tho' perhaps in a greater degree by the English than by the Dutch inhabitants, and we think that it is attributable in the latter to the interest which has been felt in two great questions upon which His Majesty's Government has decided during the last three years, to the neglect of those means which the Local Government could at one period have commanded of anticipating the extent of the present demand by a temperate and judicious use of the power which it monopolised, to the open abuse which upon one occasion was made of that power, and to the transgression of a law in another, by which the Government Press was made with impunity an instrument of attack upon the character of an individual even more unjustifiable than the former.

These circumstances were not without their weight in the recommendation which we had the honor to make in our Report upon the finances of the Colony, respecting the abolition of the Printing Establishment conducted by the Colonial Government.

But Greig's troubles were not at an end on his return from London. Although he had received compensation for the printing materials confiscated by the Government, he expected to get them back. But as they had been sold to Bridekirk, who had started an independent business with Greig's types on 30 July 1824,[1] this was not possible immediately on Greig's arrival at the Cape in August 1825. When they were offered to him in June 1826, he declined, stating that he had 'been compelled to sink capital in the purchase of a competent stock from London'.[2] One cannot but think that by this time the type would have been considerably the worse for wear, because Bridekirk had been issuing an English and Dutch weekly, the *South African Chronicle and Mercantile Advertiser*, from 18 August 1824. It was started when Greig was banished as a government-inspired publication with Richard Plasket (Secretary to the Government) and A. J. Jardine (Librarian at the South African Public Library) writing for it. It ceased publication on 26 December 1826, when Bridekirk relinquished it as a losing concern. When Greig did not take over the type which had been sold to Bridekirk, the new type which the Government had imported with the intention of letting Bridekirk have it, was diverted to the Government Printing Office.

On 7 October 1826 George Greig in the course of a letter to Sir Richard Plasket objecting to the proposed stamp duty and postage on newspapers, had much of interest to say on the cost of running a printing works in Cape Town:[3]

> I would therefore respectfully request His Honor to consider that the expences of a printing establishment at the Cape are much greater than in England. The materials have to be transported from Europe at a heavy rate of freight and insurance, and on reaching the Colony they are subjected to an additional charge of 3¼ per cent. A larger stock than is at any time in requisition must be kept on hand, in order to meet the length of time increased by the dangers of the seas which must intervene before any portion of them can be replaced. The making or repairing of such articles at the Cape costs nearly three times the London prices, yet it is often a matter of necessity to employ colonial artizans for these purposes.
>
> But it is not only the machinery of the Press, the types, paper, ink, etc. for printing that must be imported from England, at so great an expence and outlay of capital, the workmen also must be brought from the same distant quarter, a sum of about £50 must be advanced for an ordinary journeyman printer before he will leave his country, where he can always secure employment and a competent support by his profession, to commit his fortune among strangers in a colony where the press has hitherto enjoyed so precarious an existence. The rate of wages is also much higher than workmen of the same ability can obtain in the wealthiest establishments in London, while the dissipated habits which most of them acquire on their first arrival, owing to the cheap-

1. *Government Gazette*, 31 July 1824.
2. Theal, G. M. *Records of the Cape Colony, December 1826, etc.* [London ?], printed for the Government of the Cape Colony, 1905, p. 323.
3. Theal, G. M. *Records of the Cape Colony, December 1826, etc.*, p. 405–407.

ness of deleterious wine and brandy, and their insubordination, caused partly by that and partly by the absence of competition, which exposes their employers so much to their caprice, renders their average day's work considerably less than would be exacted at home. It is no uncommon thing for the correction of a column of letter press to cost nearly as much time, and consequently nearly as much additional expence (for the men are paid by the day) as the composing of the types in the first instance.

In order to cooperate with His Majesty's Government in the benevolent and useful design of encouraging reading and the study of the English language among the Dutch and the native inhabitants, I have also incurred the heavy charge and great additional trouble of printing the whole of the matter contained in my paper *in both languages*. On this account a Dutch translator and Dutch corrector of the press had to be added to the establishment. From this arrangement I have never received any pecuniary benefit, the increased expence exceeding any increase in my sales which could be ascribed to it; and I would long since have discontinued the practice had not the incalculable benefit derived from it by the old inhabitants outweighed with me every other consideration.

Now in London where none of these drawbacks and disadvantages are experienced, the proprietors of newspapers, which have a *daily* sale of from six to seven thousand copies, and which contain in their columns from 200 to 1,000 advertisements, find it necessary to charge 3d. per copy, exclusive of the stamp. How then is it supposed possible that at the Cape, under circumstances so dissimilar, a newspaper which can never reach a *sixth* part of that circulation, even *once* in the week, and which seldom receives more than 20 advertisements,—how can such a paper be issued at the price of 2½d. to which the proposed postage and stamp duty would reduce it? In what misconception could such an idea originate? Let the experiment be tried in the Cape *Gazette*. Put a postage and stamp duty upon it,deduct from the proceeds of its sales the interest of the money sunk in the establishment, the salaries of an Editor, Translator, and Superintendant, the wages of the workmen, the wear and tear of materials, house rent, insurance etc. upon goods procured from England, the payment of an agent there for transacting the business, and all other charges, and though it possesses many great advantages denied *only in this Colony* to such papers as mine, His Honor will soon be convinced of the truth of the views I have stated. In fact up to the present time the sales of the *Advertiser* have not nearly met the expenditure and risk.

On 10 March 1827 Greig was informed by the Secretary to the Government 'that in consequence of a publication in the *South African Commercial Advertiser* of Wednesday the 24th of May last, containing a statement entitled "Mr. Buissine's case", and which has been represented by His Excellency The Governor Lord Charles Somerset [then in London] to be of a false and calumnious nature, His Honor [the Lt.-Governor] has received Instructions from His Majesty's Secretary of State for the Colonies, to cancel the Licence under which you are allowed to Print and Publish that Journal'.[1]

1. Theal, G. M. *Records of the Cape Colony from February to June 1827, etc.* [London?], printed for the Government of the Cape Colony, 1905, p. 76.

Richard Bourke, Lieutenant-Governor at the time, questioned the legality of forcing anyone to obtain a licence to print a regular newspaper, and questioned whether the Proclamation issued by Sir George Yonge on 21 July 1800 would justify such an action. In any case, the offending passage had, as was the custom in the nineteenth century, been taken over just as it stood from the London *Times* where it had appeared fourteen months earlier without exciting any comment. This time John Fairbairn went to London to protest, and on the advice of Bourke, the Imperial Government agreed to a free press with a law of libel. Fairbairn told the story in *Papers explaining the Cause of Lord Bathurst's last Interference with the Press at the Cape of Good Hope, etc.* London, printed by Bagster & Thomas, 1827. Fairbairn was given permission to resume the publication of the *South African Commercial Advertiser*, and it duly appeared once more on 3 October 1828, and continued under various names, owners and editors until it was incorporated in the *Cape Standard and Mail* on 29 September 1869. The promise to Fairbairn that the press would be freed from the control of the Governor and Council was implemented by a new Ordinance published in the *Government Gazette* on 8 May 1829.

George Greig was associated with the printing of various other periodical publications issued in Cape Town. Some of them are: *Het Nederduitsch Zuid-Afrikaansche Tydschrift* (1824–1834), which succeeded in escaping Lord Charles Somerset's ire during the period of the struggle for the freedom of the press; *The New Organ* (1826) closed down after the first issue because the organizers had failed to obtain a licence; *The Colonist* (1828); *The South African Quarterly Journal* (1831–1834), the first scientific periodical issued in South Africa; *The Cape of Good Hope Literary Gazette* (1830); and *The South African Missionary Herald* (1828), presumably the earliest missionary journal published in South Africa. Pamphlets and books from his press exist in English and Dutch on a variety of subjects, and his imprint occurs on Cape Almanacs from 1828 to 1835. At the end of June 1835 Greig relinquished his personal interest in the printing business and the retail trade, and continued as a wholesaler,[1] and his imprint does not occur after 1835. There is some uncertainty about his movements in later years, nor is the exact date of his death known. It seems that he left Cape Town to reside in London in 1843,[2] but it is nevertheless on record that his tender for Cape Government printing was accepted when the Government Printing Office closed in December 1844.

1. Robinson, A. M. Lewin. *None daring to make us afraid, etc.* Cape Town, Maskew Miller, 1962, p. 111.
2. Pringle, T. *Narrative of a Residence in South Africa;* with introduction, biographical and historical notes by A. M. Lewin Robinson, *etc.* Cape Town, C. Struik, 1966, p. 343.

Broadside type specimen published by S. J. Mollett, Cape Town, in 1837, a few years after having taken o from Greig and Bridekirk. (Reduce Original in the Africana Museum, Johannesbu

Specimen.

GAZETTE & TRADE LIST

Printing Office,

No. 1, GRAVE-STREET, CAPE TOWN.

LONG PRIMER SHADED,

Pica Black,

BREVIER TUSCAN,

BREVIER NONPAREIL ANTIQUE,

NONPAREIL ROMAN AND *ITALIC.*

NONPAREIL SKELETON,

BREVIER SANSSCRIFT,

ENGLISH ORNAMENTED,

Small Pica Black.

PRINTING,

With the most modern and handsome Type, executed at the above Establishment with economy and dispatch.

Great Primer Script, for Circulars, &c.

LARGE LETTER,

SUITABLE FOR POSTERS; AND EVERY DESCRIPTION OF SMALLER TYPE FOR

Jobbing and Book Work;

TOGETHER WITH

Βρηυιερ, Λουγ Πριμερ, ανδ Πικα Γρηηκ.

Superior Letters and Figures for References, Mathematical and other Signs, &c. &c. &c.

PRINTED BY S. J. MOLLETT, AT THE GAZETTE AND TRADE LIST OFFICE.
GRAVE-STREET, CAPE TOWN, CAPE OF GOOD HOPE.
1837

On 11 September 1840 the *Gazette* carried an advertisement offering materials to book-binders by George Greig, but the same publication on 14 November 1845 offered similar materials as being available from George Greig & Co.

The quality of printing at the Cape during the first thirty years or so of the nineteenth century was generally speaking not of a high order, although occasional references are found in contemporary sources showing that the standard of printing did excite some interest. *The South African Chronicle* of 15 December 1824, for example, claimed that it was responsible for 'the improved state of letter press printing at the Cape' and stated that Cape printing was superior to that of India or New South Wales. Greig was certainly a force to be reckoned with, and a man who was not afraid of new ideas, but most of his printing is not particularly impressive or in any way distinguished. To his credit it must be said that he introduced woodcuts into the almanacs in 1830 and lithographs (made in London) in the following year. He was also responsible for the inclusion of advertisements in the rather austere almanacs in 1830.

S. J. Mollett of the Albion Press, who took over the general printing business relinquished by Greig in June 1835 and also succeeded Bridekirk at this time as printer of the *Government Gazette*, continually drew attention to his 'beautiful selection of the most modern and handsome type' which enabled him to do printing 'in the first style of the art'.[1] On 11 December 1835 Mollett informed the public that he had just received one of Hopkinson's improved Albion presses, and invited 'the curious' to come and see the 'beautiful model' which 'shows so strikingly the improvement ... in this branch of art'. On occasion a cut of a printing press was used at the head of his advertisements, as for example in the *Gazette* of 18 September 1840, where he used about a dozen different types in as many lines to illustrate the 'varied assortment of the most modern fancy and plain types' available for 'every kind of mercantile and general typography'. A specimen sheet of his dated 1837 has survived in the Africana Museum in Johannesburg, and includes Greek type.

Printing in Cape Town was certainly not always easy, as is shown by the difficulty Bridekirk experienced in 1831 in printing the first translation of the four Gospels in the language spoken by the Nama Hottentots. The note in T. H. Darlow and H. F. Moule's *Historical Catalogue of the Printed Editions of Holy Scripture, etc.* reads: 'In 1826 J. H. Schmelen had taken this translation to Capetown, but decided to post-

1. Jenkins, O. 'Our Printing Pioneers' in *The South African Printer and Stationer*, December 1939, p. 361.

pone the printing until special signs to represent the 'clicks' could be supplied. These signs were cast in England, but when they arrived at Capetown they were found to be of an unsuitable size and the book had to be printed without them.'[1] The imprint runs: 'Diihiiko Hoekaysna Kaykoep Bridekirkkipga', meaning 'Done in Cape Town by Mr. (Literally Big Master) Bridekirk'.

Cape Town printers of the first half of the nineteenth century had not only to contend with the problems encountered in setting text in African languages, but also in even less familiar tongues. In 1846, for example, they were required to print a New Testament in Land Dyak, a language of Borneo.

It is on record that in 1830 there was no Arabic type at the Cape, and a little later a Malay catechism was lithographed by M. C. Schonegevel. But in the eighteen-fifties the Rev. F. Lion Cachet is reported as having had an Arabic -Dutch reader printed 'with some difficulty'. This is but one example of a number of publications printed at the Cape in which Dutch words were printed in Arabic characters for the use of Malays and others who could read Arabic.[2]

The first weekly at the Cape printed entirely in Dutch emanated from Bridekirk's press, and was called *De Verzamelaar* (the gleaner). Its editor and proprietor was one of the Cape's most colourful figures, Josephus Suasso de Lima (1791–1858), a Dutchman of Portuguese-Jewish extraction. He arrived at the Cape in 1818, and started this journal on 7 January 1826. Because he was in favour of the Government, he escaped the sort of trouble encountered by Greig. *De Verzamelaar* (in later years bilingual) appeared irregularly from 1826 to 19 December 1848, because De Lima was always in financial trouble. De Lima's reputation rests upon his work as a writer and dramatist, but as he also owned a press, and as his name occurs in imprints, he is noted here. On one of the numerous occasions when he was in financial difficulties, his press was confiscated by his creditors and used on 9 April 1830 to start another Dutch paper, *De Zuid-Afrikaan*, under the editorship of his chief rival, C. E. Boniface. De Lima issued a series of almanacs at intervals from 1832 to 1854, and published a *Post Office and General Directory* in 1855.[3]

1. Darlow, T. H. & H. F. Moule. *Historical Catalogue of the Printed Editions of Holy Scripture in the Library of the British and Foreign Bible Society*. London, Bible House, 1903–1911, p. 1137.
2. Van Selms, A. *Arabies-Afrikaanse Studies, etc.* Amsterdam, Noord-Hollandsche Uitgevers Maatschappij, 1951.
3. Mandelbrote, J. C. 'Joseph Suasso de Lima, 1791–1856: a bibliography' in: *Quarterly Bulletin of the South African Library*, Sep. 1948, p. 2–22.

Philippus Albertus Brand (1808–1872) was a Cape Town businessman rather than a practising printer, who was associated with *De Zuid-Afrikaan*, and whose name appears in the imprint of Charles Etienne Boniface's *De Nieuwe Ridderorde; of, De Temperantisten* (The new order of chivalry) published in Cape Town in 1832 as the first known original dramatic work written in South Africa. The earliest examples of such an imprint occur in 1831 in a sermon by J. Philip entitled *The Importance of Early Instruction* and in the October and November issues of *South African Christian Recorder*, a missionary journal. Apparently Brand, on account of financial difficulties, declined the invitation of General A. W. J. Pretorius in February 1851 to start a press in the Transvaal.[1]

The Cape of Good Hope Literary Gazette of June 1835 noted the retirement of both Greig and Bridekirk and drew attention to the firm of Pike and Richert. George James Pike's name appears in Cape Town imprints from 1830 to 1859, sometimes on his own, and at other times with Richert, or Philip, or Riches. The earliest item printed by Pike is *Een Adres aan de Aandeelhouders van het Zuid Afrikaansche Athenaeum* (an address to the shareholders in the South African Athenaeum) by Dr. Adamson.[2] Among his more important works are three philological works— A. N. E. Changuion's *De Nederduitsche Taal in Zuid-Afrika Hersteld* (The Dutch language restored in South Africa) issued in 1844, as well as J. L. Döhne's *Zulu-Kafir Dictionary* and Henry Tindall's *Grammar of the Namaqua Hottentot Language*, both issued in 1857.

Laidler[3] lists Saul Solomon's name in an imprint for the first time in 1833 when listing *Kaapstad's Municipaliteit Markt Regulatiën* (Market regulations of the Cape Town Municipality). The *Cape Argus*, which Solomon printed for the first time, when it was founded on 3 January 1857, supplied the following biographical details on 27 September 1958:

> Saul Solomon was born on the island of St. Helena on May 25, 1817. His father had been put ashore there when he became ill on a voyage intended to take him to Australia from England and founded a firm of merchants. Saul was sent to a boarding school at Ramsgate, England, and it was there that he contracted rheumatic fever, which stunted the growth of his legs. He was no more than four feet in height.
>
> In 1828 he returned to St. Helena and was later sent to Cape Town to complete his education.

1. Vermooten, F. *'n Drukker-pionier: Johannes Philippus Borrius, 1840–1892:* tesis ... M. A. graad in die vak geskiedenis by die Potchefstroomse Universiteits-kollege, 1945, p. 1. [Unpublished thesis].
2. Laidler, P. W. *The Pre-Victorian Products of the Cape Press.* Johannesburg, no pub., 1935, No. 412.
3. *Ibidem*, No. 527.

In 1832 he left school and, after working for a year in a steel engraver's business, he entered the printing trade, being employed by George Greig as an apprentice bookbinder.

He eventually became a partner and later took over the establishment under the name of Saul Solomon and Company and printed the 'Government Gazette' and numerous journals.

On September 26, 1880, the greatest tragedy in Saul Solomon's life occurred when his five-year-old daughter, Maggie, was drowned in a newly built reservoir. He never fully recovered from this shock and his health deteriorated and he lost all interest in business and politics.

On July 1, 1881, Solomon sold The Argus to Francis Dormer for £6,000 and from this transaction the foundations of The Argus Company were laid.

Solomon's interests did not lie only in the printing trade. He was a keen politician. In 1854 he became a member of the first Cape Parliament and was one of the most outstanding speakers in the House. Because he was so short he stood on a footstool when he addressed the House.

Saul Solomon died aged seventy-five on 16 October 1892 while on a visit to Britain.

Many important nineteenth-century South African works in Dutch, English, and African vernacular languages after 1850 bear Solomon's imprint, as is to be expected since he soon built up the best equipped printing works in Cape Town. Early in 1854 he set up the first lithographic press of any consequence in Cape Town, as the earlier lithographic work had been done on a very small scale by amateurs or artists. On 10 August 1854 he introduced printing by steam.[1] This innovation apparently caught the popular imagination, for a well-known musician of the time, J. S. de Villiers, was responsible for *The Steam Printing Press Movement, composed in commemoration of the introduction of printing by steam*. It was published in 1855 by A. S. Robertson & Thos. Sliegh of Cape Town. The *Cape Almanac* for 1856 also noted 'printing by steam successfully accomplished by Saul Solomon & Co.'. Perhaps not so successfully accomplished, but nevertheless the task which brought world-wide fame to Saul Solomon even today (among philatelists at any rate), was the production of one penny and four-penny postage stamps for the Cape Government in 1861 when there was a shortage of these values owing to a delay in the supplies from Britain. Saul Solomon was, according to D. Alan Stevenson's authoritative work *The Triangular Stamps of Cape of Good Hope*, p. 71, entrusted with this task because he had just imported stereotyping machinery. As the engraving was done on steel, the term woodblock is, of course, a misnomer, but not surprising, considering how crude Solomon's stamps are in comparison with the originals by Perkins, Bacon & Petch.

During the middle years of the nineteenth century Solomon was associated with

1. Rosenthal, E. *160 Years of Cape Town Printing*. (Cape Town, Cape Town Association of Printing House Craftsmen and the Cape Chamber of Printing, 1960), p. 23.

Broadside type specimen published by Brink, Mollett & Co., Cape Town, in the 1850s, showing a u though not very distinguished choice of then fashionable typef (Reduced by approximately one-third.) Original in the Africana Museum, Johannesb

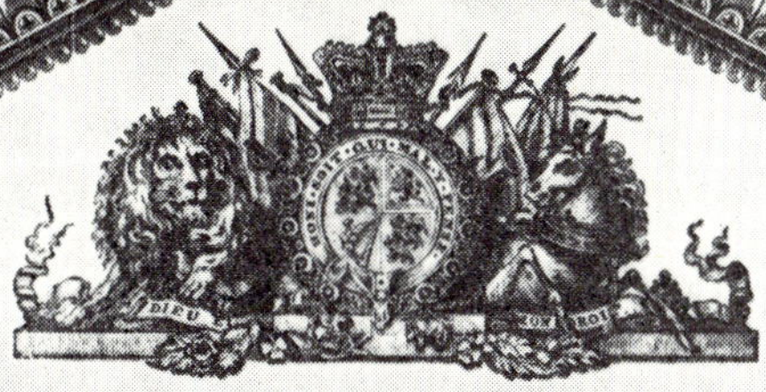

SPECIMEN.

PRINTING TYPES.

TWO-LINE BREVIER TUSCAN.

Pica, Full Face.

TWO-LINE PEARL ITALIAN.

ENGLISH ORNAMENTED, SHADED.

NONPAREIL, OUTLINE.

Long Primer, Italic, Full Face.

MINION, FULL FACE.

ENGLISH ORNAMENTED.

Two-Line Pica Script.

Long Primer Black.

BREVIER SANSERIF, OUTLINE.

PARAGON ITALIAN, SHADED.

Brevier Nonpareil Antique.

BREVIER TUSCAN, OUTLINE.

Great Primer Black, Open.

Great Primer Script.

Brevier Antique.

TWO-LINE PEARL, OUTLINE.

BREVIER TUSCAN.

Long Primer, Full Face.

TWO-LINE PEARL TUSCAN, ORNAMENTED.

BREVIER, FULL FACE.

Λογγ Πριμερ Γρηκ.

[illegible] Black, Outline.

Great Primer, Roman.—*Great Primer, Italic.*

English, Roman.—*English, Italic.*

Pica, Roman.—*Pica, Italic.*

Small Pica, Roman.—*Small Pica, Italic.*

Long Primer, Roman.—*Long Primer, Italic.*

Brevier, Roman.—*Brevier, Italic.*

Minion, Roman.—*Minion, Italic.*

Nonpareil, Roman.—*Nonpareil, Italic.*

TOGETHER WITH A VARIETY OF LARGE TYPE.

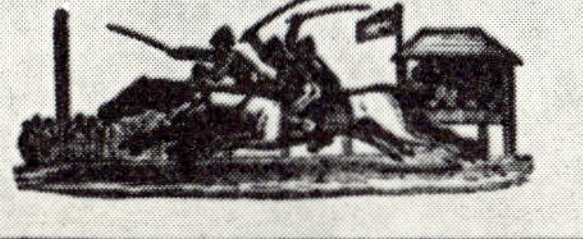

BRINK, MOLLETT, ROUBAIX, AND KEEVE,

PRINTERS,

11, St. George's Street, Cape Town.

FIRM,

BRINK, MOLLETT, & Co.

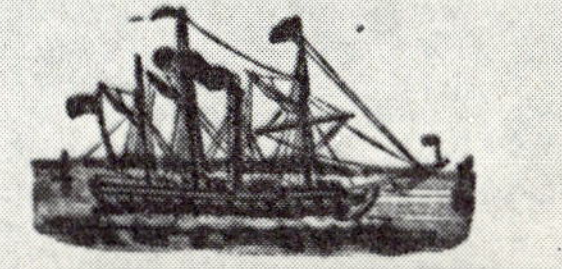

a large number of journals either as printer, publisher, or owner. A few are *Cape Mercantile Advertiser*, *Cape Monitor*, *Cape of Good Hope Exchange Gazette*, *Cape Government Gazette*, *Cape Town Mail and Mirror* and the *Church Magazine*.

In 1855 Saul Solomon provided a vade-mecum to the exhibits sent by the Cape Colony to the International Exhibition in Paris, and in 'Section A 206 Imprimerie' special mention is made of the 'première et seule presse à vapeur fonctionnant au Cap'. On view in this section, apart from the guide printed by Solomon, was Dr. L. Pappe's *Silva capensis; or, A Description of South African Forest Trees and Arborescent Shrubs, used for technical and oeconomical purposes by the Colonists of the Cape of Good Hope.*[1] This pamphlet was printed in 1854 by Van de Sandt de Villiers & Co. of Cape Town.

The name B. J. van de Sandt de Villiers harks back to the first South African born printer, Bernardus Josephus van de Sandt (1799–1850). His wife was Susanna Johanna de Villiers, and as they had no children, Van de Sandt adopted the son of his wife's brother, P. J. A. de Villiers. This son, born in 1826, was first known as B. J. van de Sandt, Junior, but in 1847, when he came of age, he became known as B. J. van de Sandt de Villiers. He was educated by his uncle and apprenticed to the Government Printing Office. His earliest imprints read B. J. van de Sandt, Junior, but from 1850 his business became known as Van de Sandt de Villiers & Co.[2]

From 1851 to 1862 the *Cape Almanacs* bear his name, and he was associated with religious journals such as the *Kerkbode* (Church messenger) and *Elpis*, but his main claim to fame is that he was concerned in establishing the liberal newspaper *Het Volksblad* (The people's paper) in 1849 at the time of the anti-convict agitation, when both the English and the Dutch were strongly opposed to using the Cape as a penal settlement. In his obituary *The Cape Argus* of 9 April 1878 refers to his partnership first with J. G. Tier and later with J. D. Marquard, presumably a relative of his wife, Albertina Marquard. His son-in-law, James Frederick Centlivres, succeeded to the business.

In passing it should be noted that Van de Sandt de Villiers printed music in 1852, and Saul Solomon in 1846 and 1854 .The first known South African music printing was a Dutch hymn tune by F. Logier printed by the Gazette Office in 1840. Dr.

1. *Exposition universelle, 1855: Colonie du Cap de Bonne Espérance: Vadé-mécum, etc.* Cape Town, Saul Solomon, 1855, p. 77.
2. Smit, J. B. *Bibliografie van die Drukpers-maatskappy van B. J. van de Sandt de Villiers.* [Cape Town, University of Cape Town, School of Librarianship, 1946?]. p. i–iii. [Unpublished].

F. Z. van der Merwe noted that it was set in ordinary letterpress, as the compositor obviously had no music type.[1]

The *Cape Almanac* for 1845 records nine printing establishments in Cape Town and Suasso de Lima's *Census* of 1855 notes forty-three compositors, nine pressmen, five printing offices and an additional one, 'Printing Office—Steam' for Saul Solomon. It is therefore not surprising to find the 1842 edition of the *Almanac* noting the existence of The Cape of Good Hope Printers' Protection Society, established under the sanction of the Governor, Sir George Napier, on 5 July 1841. The first officials were: President: S. Brink, with J. Coenradie as Vice-President; J. C. Eckley as Treasurer, with J. Bathie as Secretary, and R. L. Keeve as Steward. This, it is believed, was the first trade union to be established in South Africa. The 'Prospectus addressed to the Journeymen Printers of Cape Town' can still be seen in the Cape Archives.

On 21 March 1857 a Printers' and Bookbinders' Mutual Benefit Society was established in Cape Town. The *Cape Almanac* for 1860 lists G. D. Rodger as President, J. W. Barnett as Vice-President. The objects of the Society were very much the same as those of similar societies today. Neither the trade union nor the benefit society seems to have survived for any length of time.

In 1852 when Dean Newman addressed the Annual Meeting of the South African Public Library on 8 May on the 'Art of Printing', no mention whatsoever was made of a single item printed at the Cape. Yet in *Gazette* of 12 August 1825, Howell, the Cape Town bookseller, listed publications of the Cape press. Today every scrap that issued from these presses, particularly before 1850, is treasured by collectors all over South Africa.

1. Van der Merwe, F. Z. *Suid-Afrikaanse-Musiekbibliografie, 1787–1952.* Pretoria, J. L. van Schaik, 1958, p. 18.

Mission Presses

Missionaries have been working among the peoples of South Africa since 1737, and from the early days the Protestant missions in particular have been active in supplying reading matter for the use of their converts. In almost every case, particularly in the early years of any mission, the missionary himself had first to learn the language, reduce it to writing, translate the Scriptures, write original matter for teaching purposes, himself learn to print, obtain the necessary materials, and finally among his multifarious other duties, keep a printing press going, possibly with a little help from members of his congregation whom he had first taught to read and write, and then to print. And all this frequently happened in the most remote parts of the country miles away from any source of supply.

Dr. J. T. van der Kemp and J. Read, missionaries of the London Missionary Society, were at Graaff Reinet in May 1801, and it is believed that they were responsible for the first printing in South Africa outside Cape Town. Under 24 June 1801 in the *Transactions of the Missionary Society*, p. 481 it is recorded that they printed four hundred copies of a spelling table, and on 11 November 1801 Van der Kemp wrote to Gen. Dundas from Graaff Reinet to say: 'The number of children in our reading-school amounts to one hundred and twelve, of whom, however, seldom more than seventy are present. We have been obliged to print a spelling-book for their use, and we hope that Your Excellency will permit us to print and to sell little school-books, for the benefit of the future establishment, and to educate some of our young men in the art of printing.'[1] Unfortunately neither table nor spelling book has survived. Nor has a copy been found of Dr. Van der Kemp's so-called Bethelsdorp catechism of 1804,[2] although collectors have been searching at

1. Philip, J. *Researches in South Africa, etc.* London, James Duncan, 1828, vol. 1, p. 76.
2. Varley, D. H. 'The Bethelsdorp Catechism of 1804' in *Africana Notes and News*, vol. 4, No. 1, Dec. 1946, p. 3–8.

least since Dr. W. H. I. Bleek began collecting the products of South African mission presses in the middle years of the nineteenth century for the Governor, Sir George Grey.

Bethelsdorp was visited by Dr. Heinrich Lichtenstein, when he accompanied the Commissioner De Mist on his journey into the interior in 1803 and 1804, and later, when the missionary was in Cape Town, Lichtenstein saw much of him. He was therefore in a position to know about Dr. Van der Kemp's activities. Consequently one accepts Lichtenstein's statement that Van der Kemp printed a catechism in the Hottentot language for the use of the missionaries.[1] The title is given by the philologist, Dr. W. H. I. Bleek,[2] as *Tzitzika Thuickwedi mika khwekhwenama*, meaning 'Principles of the Word of God for the Hottentot Nation.'

The kind of problems which beset missionary printers can be gauged from the fate of the printing press which was sent out from London, and arrived safely in Cape Town, where it was trans-shipped in the coasting vessel *John* bound for Algoa Bay, being intended for Bethelsdorp. Unfortunately the vessel foundered on 16 September 1803, and so Dr. Van der Kemp did not receive the longed-for press, or as the London Missionary Society *Report* for 1805 (p. 10) reads: 'Our brethren were also disappointed in their expectation of receiving a printing press.'

Although Dr. Van der Kemp died in Cape Town on 15 December 1811, printing continued at Bethelsdorp, a printing office and a school room measuring 70×80 feet being built in 1816; a new press being sent out from London in 1822; and a small printing office in 1827 making it possible to print elementary books.

The Rev. John Campbell, who visited South Africa on behalf of the London Missionary Society from 24 October 1812 to 13 February 1814, tells of the Boer who, on seeing Dr. Van der Kemp's printing press, enquired what it was. When the use of the press had been explained, the Doctor was asked to have a large folio Bible with plates ready for him by the next day.[3] Not an improbable story in a country with only one press in Cape Town and another at a mission station some five hundred miles away.

Robert Moffat (1795–1883) is generally remembered as the translator of the Bible into Tswana and as David Livingstone's father-in-law. He also figures in the

1. Lichtenstein, H. *Travels in Southern Africa in the Years 1803, 1804, 1805 and 1806* ... a reprint of the translation ... by Anne Plumptre. Cape Town, Van Riebeeck Society, 1930, V. 2, p. 465 n.
2. Bleek, W. H. I. *The Library of ... Sir George Grey: Philology: V. I, pt. 1: South Africa.* London, Trübner, 1858, Item 30.
3. Campbell, J. *Travels in South Africa, etc.* London, printed for the Author by T. Rutt, 1815, p. 533.

history of mission printing in South Africa, because of his work at Kuruman, known as (New) Lattakoo by nineteenth-century travellers, many of whom spent a considerable time at this mission station (or village) run by the London Missionary Society. By 1830 Moffat was in Cape Town to have his Tswana translation of parts of the Bible printed. No Cape Town printer was at that time in a position to undertake Moffat's translation of the Gospel of Luke or the hymn book he had prepared. He was finally allowed to use the Government Printing Office and given a printer to assist him. They printed a thousand copies of *Luke*. Moffat tells the story as follows in his *Missionary Labours and Scenes in Southern Africa* published in London by John Snow in 1842 (p. 562–563):

> After arriving at Graham's Town, where I left my family while I visited several of the missionary stations in Kaffirland, and then some of those within the Colony, we reached Cape Town in October, 1830. From the infant state of typography in that place, I found it necessary to apply to Sir Lowry Cole, then governor, to allow the Gospel of Luke to be printed at the government printing office. This request was cheerfully acceded to, but compositors were wanted. This circumstance, with the promise of an excellent printing press, which Dr. Philip had in his possession for our mission, was a strong inducement for me to learn printing; and being joined by Mr. Edwards, who was originally destined to the Bechuana mission, and now appointed to go there, the work was completed under the kind superintendence of Mr. Van der Zandt. [i.e. B. J. van de Sandt]. The paper was supplied by the British and Foreign Bible Society, by whom also other incidental expenses were defrayed, which was only a precursor of the boon since conferred by that noble institution on the Bechuana mission, the fruits of which will be reaped by generations yet unborn. A small hymn-book was also printed in the language.

Moffat was back in Kuruman by June 1831, his press set up by 15 September, and his story on page 564 continues:

> ... the press was soon called into operation, when lessons, spelling books, and catechisms were prepared for the schools. Although many of the natives had been informed how books were printed, nothing could exceed their surprise when they saw a white sheet, after disappearing for a moment, emerge spangled with letters. After a few noisy exclamations, one obtained a sheet with which he bounded into the village, showing it to every one he met, and asserting that Mr. Edwards and I had made it in a moment, with a round black hammer (a printer's ball) and a shake of the arm. The description of such a juggling process, soon brought a crowd to see the 'segatisho', (press) which has since proved an auxiliary of vast importance to our cause.

Moffat also recalled in later years that a Miss Lees of Manchester collected sufficient money to purchase a small fount of type for the mission. Robert Moffat and R. Edwards printed *Buka ea Pocho ea Tuto le Poluko tsa Yesu Keresta* (a catechism) before the end of the year on the press at Kuruman, and in 1835 finished the last twenty-four pages of the hymn book started in Cape Town in 1831.

As always with mission presses in far-distant places, there was the problem of getting supplies, including paper. Moffat tells (p. 570) how Mrs. Moffat journeyed to the Eastern Province on her own to see their children at school at Salem. On her return in November 1833, after an absence of five months, she brought a supply of paper and large type furnished by the London Missionary Society. Moffat relates that they flattered themselves that their school books were well printed, and draws attention to the slowness of printing because they lacked type and dependable compositors. This was as late as 1851. William Ashton assisted Moffat both in printing and translating from about this period, and finally the task of translating the whole Bible into Tswana was completed, and much of it printed at Kuruman by 1857. This was the first South African vernacular to have a complete translation of the Bible, and only the third in any African language—indeed a remarkable achievement considering that Moffat did not arrive at Kuruman until 1821, and then had to learn the language and reduce it to writing. Printing continued at Kuruman after Moffat's return to Europe in 1870.

In July 1916 the original hand-press used at Kuruman was transferred as a museum piece to the Kimberley Public Library. One can but wonder if this was the press W. A. Hankey, the Treasurer of the London Missionary Society, had in mind when he sought permission from Earl Bathurst on 15 March 1825 to send a press to the Cape for the exclusive use of the mission for the printing of books of religious and other types of instruction. Cecil Northcott in *Robert Moffat: Pioneer in Africa 1817–1870*, published by the Lutterworth Press in 1961 (p. 341) implies that it was.

The story of mission presses in South Africa abounds in problems. One of these is the question whether there ever was a press at Griquatown, for the only reference to any publications occurs in W. H. I. Bleek's Catalogue to the collection brought together for Sir George Grey, and the 'Sechuana spelling book' itself has not been traced in the South African Public Library. It has been suggested that if there had been a press at Griquatown, Moffat would surely not have journeyed first to Port Elizabeth and then to Cape Town in search of a printer for his Tswana translation of Luke in 1830. True as this may be, it is still possible that Griquatown, established as a mission station in 1802, may have had a press on which the lost spelling book could have been printed in 1821. This possibility can certainly not be excluded in the light of the following.

The *Report* of the Directors of the London Missionary Society dated 14 May 1818 (p. 33) refers to a printing press intended for Lattakoo being in use at Griquatown where 'the missionaries have begun to compile a dictionary and a catechism in the Bootsuana language.' And then silence, it seems, except for a note dated 5 July 1819 from W. Anderson (1769–1852) of Griquatown to the L.M.S. mentioning that H. Helm (1780–1884) was printing a few copies of a spelling book.

So much for printing by the London Missionary Society. The Scottish missionaries were the next to print. Chumie, a mission station on the Gwali River between Alice and Seymour, dates from 1820. The Reverend John Ross brought a small Ruthven press with him from overseas, and on 17 December 1823 the press was ready; on the 18th the alphabet was set up, and on the 19th fifty copies were 'thrown off' to quote John Bennie to Dr. Love on 20 December 1823.[1] The *South African Commercial Advertiser* of 3 March 1824, presumably referred to this publication as 'the first sheet of an elementary school book in the Caffer language', and the missionaries responsible for the work belonged to the Glasgow Missionary Society. It is believed that the place Gwali, which also occurs, was situated on the same site as Chumie, and these names seem to have been used indiscriminately in the early days.[2]

In November 1824 John Ross and John Bennie started a new mission some distance away near the Ncera River. In 1826 this station was named Lovedale, and in that year John Bennie's *A Systematic Vocabulary of the Kaffrarian Language* was printed. The Ruthven press was used both at Chumie and at Old Lovedale and utterly destroyed in the war of 1834–5. A new press sent from Britain in 1839 was operated mostly at Chumie. Chalmers printed the journal *Ikwezi* (Morning Star) on it in 1844–1845. It was a larger press than the Ruthven, possibly an Albion, and was, according to Tiyo Soga, destroyed in the War of the Axe, while the type was converted into bullets by the military. It is said that some parts of the press were found in modern times among the ruins and treasured at Lovedale. In 1836 the mission was moved to another site, and the first became known as 'Old Lovedale'.

Yet another move took place before what is the Lovedale of today was established in 1837.[3] It was only in 1861 that: William Govan on his own initiative opened a printing and bookbinding establishment at the present-day Lovedale. From the

1. Shepherd, R. H. W. *Lovedale South Africa, etc.* Lovedale, Lovedale Press, (pref. 1940), p. 62–63.
2. *Ibidem*, p. 19.
3. Cory, G. E. *The Rise of South Africa, etc.* London, Longmans, Green, 1919, V. 3, p. 197–198 n.

first, Lovedale emphasized quality of printing rather than cheapness to the user.[1]

A monthly journal, partly in Xhosa and partly in English was started in August 1862 and lasted until February 1865. It was called *Indaba* (the news), was edited by the Rev. Bryce Ross, and printed under the supervision of Wm. Govan. The *Kafir Express* was started as a monthly in 1870 in English and Xhosa. In 1876 the African section became *Isigidimi Sama-Xosa* (the Xhosa messenger), which ran for eighteen years. The English section became the *Christian Express* in 1876 and continued into the present century.

The *Pilgrim's Progress* of John Bunyan was translated 'into fluent and idiomatic Kafir'[2] and given to the Free Church of Scotland to print at Lovedale in 1867 by the translator, Tiyo Soga, one of the first educated Africans in the country. The Religious Tract Society presented the illustrations.[3] A second edition was printed during the period when George McCall Theal, the South African historian, was on the staff at Lovedale as teacher-printer from 1871 to 1878. While in charge of the printing plant, he himself printed some of his own works, as he had done previously in King William's Town, where his first work, *South Africa as it is*, was 'compiled and printed by George M. Theal, Alexandra Road, King William's Town, 1871'. The advertisement in the booklet records that 'as originally prepared it would have been three times as large, but a difficulty arose with regard to printing it. The only press obtainable was an old shattered wooden one, known on the frontier as 'Gutenberg's Original', and the type, some that was condemned years ago in a newspaper office'.[4] One can but speculate on the origins of this press.

Although the Wesleyan missionaries actually arrived before the Presbyterians, they started printing later, but were probably more active in this sphere than any other mission group in the early years. A correspondent writing in *The South African Chronicle* of 5 December 1826, who signed himself 'A Wesleyan', stated that the Wesleyans used a small Press of their own. As Barnabas Shaw, the Wesleyan missionary in Cape Town at the time, wrote the following week to say that the correspondent could not be a Wesleyan, too much credence cannot be put on this

1. Shepherd, R. H. W. *Lovedale South Africa, etc.* Lovedale, Lovedale Press, (pref. 1940), p. 400–401.
2. Du Plessis, J. *A History of Christian Missions in South Africa;* facsimile reprint [of the 1911 edition]. Cape Town, C. Struik, 1965, p. 360.
3. Chalmers, John A. *Tiyo Soga: a Page of South African Mission Work.* Edinburgh, Andrew Elliot, 1877, p. 340.
4. Mendelssohn, S. *South African Bibliography, etc.* London, Kegan Paul, Trench, Trübner, 1910, vol. 2, p. 472.

statement that there was a Wesleyan press in South Africa at this date. The quarterly paper of the Wesleyan missionary committee for December 1833 included the sentence: 'As the Wesleyan missionary committee recently sent out a suitable press, which is already fully employed at Graham's Town, in printing portions of Scripture and elementary works, under the gratuitous superintendence of a gentleman everyway qualified, nothing more is wanting, but a grant of paper from the Bible Society, to cause the printing of the Scriptures in a language known to be spoken by considerably more than half a million people.'[1] The assumption therefore is that the Wesleyans received their first press in 1833, put it at Grahamstown, and immediately set to work, for in this year St. Luke's Gospel, translated into Xhosa by W. B. Boyce, appeared. It is on record that in 1831 the British and Foreign Bible Society, in answer to a request from the Rev. William Shaw, of the Albany district, for aid in printing the Scriptures, resolved to authorize its South African Auxiliary to print at its expense an edition of 1,000 copies of the New Testament or any parts thereof. While waiting for the reply, which miscarried (not an unusual occurrence), the Wesleyan missionaries printed the Gospel according to St. Luke at Grahamstown.[2] The title reads: *I-Gospel, ezindaba ezilungileyo; ebalwe gu-Luke*, and the imprint: 'Ishicilelwe Esishicilelweni Samawesli: Erini, Graham's Town, 1833'. Erini is the Xhosa name for Grahamstown. This practice of using African vernacular place-names in imprints has caused bibliographers difficulty in identifying the place of publication of works printed in some of the lesser-known mission stations. A list of identifications by Dr. A. M. Lewin Robinson was published in *Africana Notes and News in December* 1952.[3]

Dr. H. Bennett, Medical Superintendent at Mount Coke, in September 1958, provided an extract from a letter written to the Missionary Secretaries by the Rev. W. J. Shrewsbury from Grahamstown on 7 August 1833, which indicates some of the problems with which the earlier printers of African vernaculars were faced:

> When I last wrote, I did not send you a correct statement of the quantity of type requisite to make our press complete. I misunderstood one of our friends, who is a printer, and gratuitously superintends the youths in our office, and have now obtained from him a written account of what is necessary to prevent any further error. We want—

1. Shaw, B. *Memorials of South Africa, etc.* London, J. Mason, 1840, p. 292–293.
2. Darlow, T. H., & H. F. Moule, *Historical Catalogue of the Printed Editions of Holy Scripture in the Library of the British and Foreign Bible Society*. London, Bible House, 1903–1911, p. 1695.
3. Robinson, A. M. L. 'Vernacular Place-Names in Imprints: a tentative list' in *Africana Notes and News*, vol. 10, p. 31–32.

1. *Pica* sufficient for two sheets. But as about every *tenth* or *twelfth* letter in Caffre is a *K*, a very large number of the letter K must be provided; as also a more than usual proportion of the letters B, S, X, and Z and L—say, double the quantity usually required in an English press. But the K ought to be increased *five-fold.*
2. A small Font of Pica Italic.
3. About 20 lengths of brass rule.
4. About 50 figures of each number from 1–9 and 0; also a few fractions small Pica.
5. A small quantity of small bordering for cards.
6. A cask of printers ink.

In 1834 a very important publication, *A Grammar of the Kaffir Language*, by William B. Boyce was issued by the Wesleyan Missionary Press. It marked a new era in linguistic study in South Africa, and was prepared by Boyce at the lonely mission station of Buntingville, where, as William Shaw remarked, 'he was unmarried and unencumbered with distracting cares'. After long research, Boyce discovered the key to the structure of the family of Bantu languages. The story goes that one day he was repeating aloud words and sentences that the ear might aid the eye, when in a sudden flash of perception he saw that the structure of the language was governed by a law that he felt sure was the missing key. Greatly startled were the Natives who happened to be near when the usually sedate Umfundisi [Missionary] ran capering out of the hut shouting at the top of his voice 'Eureka! Eureka!' What Boyce had discovered was that in the Kafir sentences the noun was the governing element and that all other parts of speech were thrown immediately into an alliterative or euphonic concord with the subject noun. He named the principle the 'Euphonic Concord'. That day the foundation of all subsequent study of the Bantu family of languages was well and truly laid.[1] These principles were embodied in the *Grammar* which was carefully printed on good paper. This was the first grammar of a South African Bantu language, and it stimulated not only the translation of the Scriptures, but also the provision of other reading matter in Xhosa. *Umshumaydi Wendaba* (the publisher of news) ran from July 1837 to April 1841, and is the first Xhosa journal. The first seven issues were printed at the Wesleyan Press in Grahamstown, and thereafter at Fort Peddie. It would seem that an edition of three hundred copies was published.

One of the rare references to non-whites who were employed as assistants to the missionary printers, occurs in the *Report* of the Grahamstown Auxiliary to the British and Foreign Bible Society dated 1 December 1835. It concerns the Wesleyan

1. Eveleigh, William. *The Story of a Century, 1823–1923, etc.* Cape Town, Methodist Publishing House, 1923, p. 40.

Mission Press in Grahamstown and reads: 'The printers are well acquainted with the Kafir language, one of whom is a Kafir youth, who has made considerable progress in the art of printing, during the five months he has been employed at the press.'

In 1823 the Wesleyans established a mission station north of the Vaal River at a place called Maquassi near the present-day Transvaal town of Klerksdorp. At that time no white man had settled in the area, and it was so wild, that when some of the inhabitants saw the missionaries in their wagon, they fled in terror, and told their countrymen that they had seen houses walking full of white devils. Nevertheless the missionaries, Samuel Broadbent and T. L. Hodgson, quickly learnt the language of the Barolong people and reduced it to printed form. It is recorded that a Mr. Levick of Sheffield sent a case of type, some ink, and printing balls. With these aids Broadbent printed the alphabet and words of three letters for use in the school.[1]

Owing to ill-health, Broadbent left Maquassi, and Hodgson was sent to Cape Town. During their absence, Maquassi was burnt to the ground by marauding bands. However, in 1825, Hodgson returned accompanied by the missionary James Archbell (1798–1866), who had arrived in Cape Town with his wife in 1819 and spent most of the intervening years among the peoples of Great Namaqualand. Archbell brought a small press with him and also some type. T. L. Hodgson tells the following tale:

> Seeing therefore no chance of returning to Makwasse at that time, and fearing that our health would suffer by continuing to remove from place to place, as we had done for months previously—we resolved upon building ourselves a temporary habitation in which to reside during the winter months, and thus obtain access to our books, and enjoy some measure of domestic comfort. In this temporary dwelling, Mr. Archbell got to work with the press, striking off a small elementary book in the Sichuana language.[2]

In this mud-walled cottage, where the missionaries halted on their way from Maquassi to Platberg (near the present-day Warrenton) Archbell (who later played a not unimportant part in South African history) printed the first book ever printed in the Transvaal. This must have been before 6 June 1826, for on that date the missionaries wrote; 'The small elementary book in the Sichuana language ... will show that difficulties have been conquered in the language ... and until circumstances will allow of the mission being carried on with effect, the book shall be used in the

1. Whiteside, J. *History of the Wesleyan Methodist Church of South Africa.* London, Elliot Stock, 1906, p. 329–330.
2. Hodgson, T. L. *Memoirs of Mrs. Anne Hodgson, etc.* London, J. Mason, 1836, p. 179–180.

open air, with as many children as we can collect together.'[1] The fifteen-page booklet carried the imprint 'Maquasse, 1826', but no copy is known to exist. Bibliographic references to this publication—formerly considered the first in the Tswana language—make much of the fact that it was printed in roman characters. One can but surmise that there is some reference intended to Dr. Van der Kemp's idea of using Arabic characters for African vernacular languages, or to G. F. Wrede's practice of using Greek letters for Hottentot. This information about the item printed at Maquassi ultimately derives from *Missionary Reports of the Wesleyan Methodist Society*, December 1826. When the Barolong and the missionaries reached Platberg on the Vaal, Archbell continued printing vocabularies, primers and hymns, and on 20 March 1832 he asked for a larger press and more type.[2]

The missionary John Edwards who arrived in 1832 brought a new press to Algoa Bay from where it was taken to the interior by ox wagon, first to Platberg on the Vaal and then, in 1833, to the new mission station, also called Platberg, but situated near Thaba 'Nchu. This press, according to the Medical Superintendent of the Mount Coke Hospital on 25 July 1958, was at that time being preserved in the Moroka Institution at Thaba 'Nchu, after it had been discovered by the Rev. Trevor Sadler in 1942. It had been last used by Joel Goronyani, an African, who had been trained by Edwards, and is an old Albion Press.

Richard Giddy (1806–1881) a missionary, who was also a trained printer, took charge of the press in 1837, and was pleased with the press he found on arrival, although he remarked that the type was small in quantity but in a tolerably good condition.[3] A large number of publications in various African languages, and in Dutch, were printed by Giddy, who found some of the languages, such as Koranna, difficult because they had clicks which he could indicate only by arbitrary signs. This mission station was not evacuated during the troubles of 1851 and 1852, and Giddy, risking his life, went on printing for other missionary societies during this period. There is a record of at least one occasion when this Mission press printed orders and despatches for the military in the war of 1851–52.[4] During later years the

1. Venter, I. S. J. 'Die Rol van die Drukpers in die Wesleyaanse Betsjoeanasending gedurende die Halfeeu 1825–1875' in *Historia*, September 1955, p. 162.
2. *Ibidem*, p. 163.
3. Moister, William. *Missionary Worthies: being brief memorial sketches, etc.* London, T. Woolmer, 1885, p. 358.
4. King, W. R. *Campaigning in Kaffirland; or, Scenes and Adventures in the Kaffir War of 1851–2.* London, Saunders and Otley, 1853, p. 321.

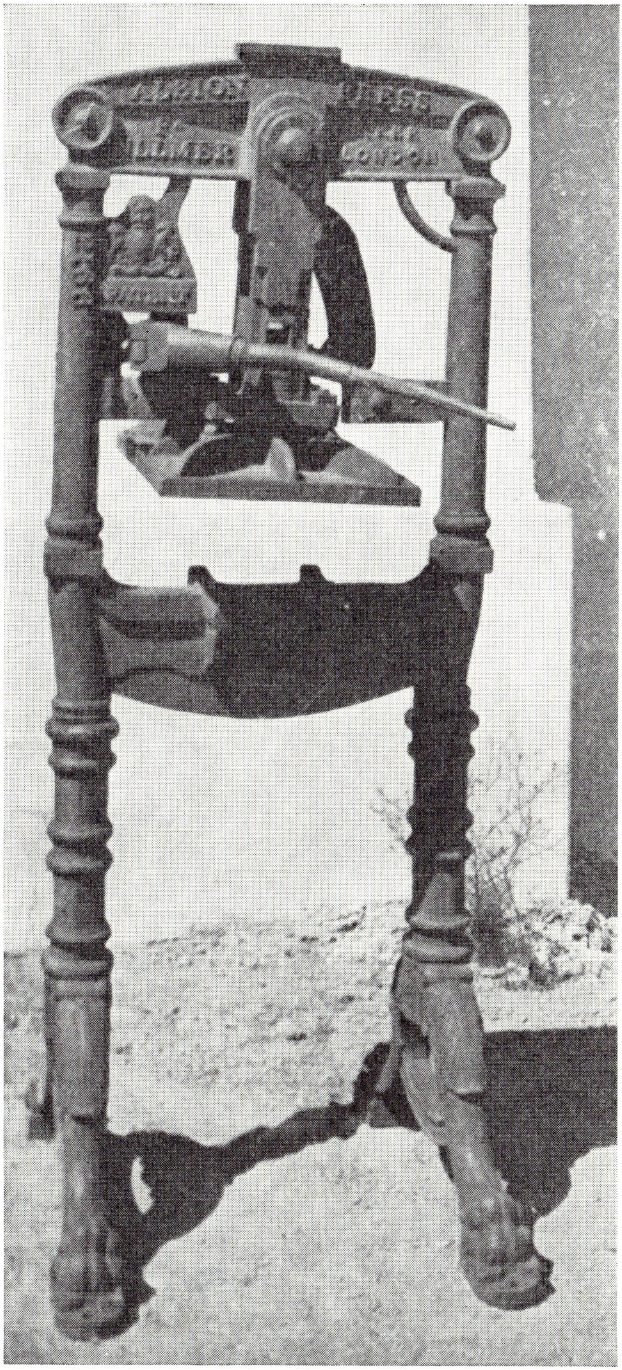

John Edwards's Albion press, used by him at the Platberg mission post since 1832, after its rediscovery in 1942. Now in the Maroka Institution at Thaba 'Nchu.

press was sometimes housed at Platberg and sometimes at Thaba 'Nchu, and both names occur in imprints.

Although Archbell, and later Giddy, printed texts as fast as they could, at least two stories about the mission stations in this area vividly illustrate the need for reading matter. John Edwards[1] who was working at Lishuani near the Basutoland border in 1833, tells how he had to improvise: 'To make a kind of alphabet and an elementary spelling book, I took some pieces of wood and cut off the ends, after making them smooth. Then with a pen-knife I carved out all the letters of the alphabet on sticks, after which the letters were dipped in ink, and stamped out on a sheet of foolscap paper. This was hung up in the reed and pole building, and the children being formed in a semicircle, I pointed out the letters to them with a long stick.'

Towards the end of 1838 the Rev. J. Allison, who was working at a station called Imperani, was engaged in translating parts of the Bible into a dialect of Sotho for Giddy to print. A letter from Allison to Giddy included the following passage: 'I received your proof-sheets, but such is the eagerness of the young people to read, that it was some time before I could get them out of their hands to mark the necessary corrections.'[2]

Printing went on at these missions until the time arrived when it became cheaper to print African vernacular publications in England. Then the Wesleyans closed down not only Thaba 'Nchu, but also their other well-known press at Mount Coke.

This station was first established in 1823 but owing to wartime troubles, it was destroyed on various occasions, moved from its original site, and finally established in 1848, approximately twelve miles east of King William's Town near the Buffalo River. The African name is Emkangiso. It was to this station the Wesleyans removed their press from King William's Town in 1853. From the records it would seem that the Wesleyans had one press in the Eastern Cape area with which they started printing in Grahamstown, as noted above, and then moved it from place to place—hence the imprints for Fort Peddie, Newtondale, Wesleyville, King William's Town, Mount Coke, Healdtown, and finally Grahamstown again, where it was closed down after 1876.

1. Edwards, J. *Fifty Years of Mission Life in South Africa*. London, T. Woolmer, 1886, p. 92.
2. Venter, I. S. J. 'Die Rol van die Drukpers in die Wesleyaanse Betsjoeanasending gedurende die Halfeeu 1825–1875' in *Historia*, September 1955, p. 165 *(quoting from Manuscript Minute Book of the Bechuana District Meetings, 1837–1850*. Thaba 'Nchu, 10.1.1838, art. 24).

The first move was in 1840 to D'Urban near Fort Peddie where J. Harvey was engaged as printer. He probably was the Job Harvey recorded as the first apprentice taken on in the office of the *Grahamstown Journal* towards the end of 1831[1] and as associated with A. Aldum, the printer of the *Cape of Good Hope Eastern Districts Government Gazette* in 1838. A primer and a translation of Proverbs are known with a Fort Peddie (or Nqushwa) imprint, and the first bears the date 1840.[2]

Newtondale (or Emtati) figures in the imprints of various Wesleyan missionary publications issued in 1844. It was while the press was at Newtondale that the Rev. John Whittle Appleyard was put in charge, and remained in this position until shortly before his death on 4 April 1874 in King William's Town. From his tombstone in King William's Town Dr. A. W. Burton, some years ago, recorded that this Wesleyan missionary had been born in Cirencester, Gloucestershire, on 15 June 1814. Thornley Smith noted[3] that after leaving Kingswood, Appleyard was bound apprentice to Mr. Joseph Wan, bookseller and printer of Shepton Mallet. From 21 January 1840 Appleyard was working as a missionary in South Africa, learning both Dutch and Xhosa. He married Miss Archbell in 1841,[4] and published the first edition of the whole of the New Testament in Xhosa at Newtondale in 1846. It was sold unbound for one shilling, bound for three shillings and sixpence, and for four shillings and sixpence it was obtainable in calf. The British and Foreign Bible Society contributed £1,000 and several grants of paper.[5]

When the War of the Axe (1846–1847) broke out, the press was immediately moved to Grahamstown for safety. At the conclusion of hostilities it went to Wesleyville.[6] As it remained here only for a short period, the assumption is that nothing of importance was printed, as no record of this place-name in an imprint has been traced. The next move was to King William's Town, where a suitable building had been acquired. Of this press Thomas Baines wrote as follows in his

1. *The Critic* (Johannesburg), 17 April 1896, p. 645.
2. Hahn, Th. *An Index of the Grey Collection in the South African Public Library*. Cape Town, Saul Solomon, 1884, p. 110, No. 12.
3. Smith, Thornley. *Memoir of the Rev. John Whittle Appleyard, Wesleyan Missionary in South Africa, etc.* London, Wesleyan Missionary Society, 1881, p. 4.
4. Uys, E. F. 'Die Mount Coke-Sendingstasie en eerw. J. W Appleyard se Xhosa-Bybelvertaling' in *Historia*, March 1961, p. 40.
5. Bleek, W. H. I. *The Library of His Excellency Sir George Grey ... Philology vol. I, pt. 1: South Africa, etc.* London, Trübner, 1858, No. 134.
6. Walker, J. A. *A Study of certain Aspects of the Mount Coke Missionary Institution:* thesis submitted as part requirement for Part II of the Bachelor of Divinity Degree, Rhodes University, Grahamstown, S.A. 1955. p. 96 [Unpublished].

journal under 8 August 1849 in describing King Williams' Town: 'A Wesleyan chapel, and in connexion with it a printing office from which, besides a newspaper in the Kafir language, the Isitunny-wa Sennyanga, or Monthly Messenger, and some periodicals ... have issued volumes that would not have disgraced any establishment in the Colony.'[1] Baines was slightly at fault in describing the Xhosa publication as a newspaper. It was a rather more ambitious monthly and included some English. The circulation was more or less eight hundred a month. It ran from August to December 1850, and was discontinued on account of the war. The press also stopped but Appleyard continued with his translation of the Bible, so that he would have copy ready when the press was again in operation. It was decided to move both Appleyard and the press to Mount Coke in 1853. The war and the move to Mount Coke probably account for the puzzling difference in place of printing on the title-page and on the last page of Appleyard's Xhosa translation of Chronicles issued in 1851/55 and of the revised edition of his Old Testament in 1853/54. On the verso of the half-title in each case King William's Town appears as the place of printing and on the title-page, in its Xhosa form of Eqonci. On the last page in both cases Emkangiso, *i.e.* Mount Coke is given. The assumption is that part of the work was done in King William's Town, and interrupted by the War and the move to Mount Coke, where the printing of this, the most important publication, was resumed and completed.

The Rev. William Shaw visited Mount Coke in October 1853 and was delighted with what he saw being printed in the way of primers, hymn books, prayer books, catechisms, and parts of the Bible.[2] He also recorded that Appleyard had to live in part of the building in which the press was housed, as his dwelling was still being built. By this time, according to J. A. Walker,[3] the press was becoming worn, and parts required replacing. Supplies were slow in coming in, and materials were not of a high quality, so that the output was not regular. Appleyard had other worries too as can be seen from his letter of 26 November 1856:[4]

1. Baines, Thomas. *Journal of Residence in Africa*, 1842–1853 ... ed. with intro., notes and map, by R. F. Kennedy. Cape Town, The Van Riebeeck Society, 1961, vol. 1, p. 131.
2. Shaw, Wm. *Memoir* ... ed. by his oldest surviving friend. London, Wesleyan Conference Office, 1874, p. 234.
3. Walker, J. A., *A Study of certain Aspects of the Mount Coke Missionary Institution:* thesis submitted as part requirement for Part II of the Bachelor of Divinity Degree, Rhodes University, Grahamstown, S.A., 1955, p. 98. [Unpublished].
4. Smith, Thornley, *Memoir of the Rev. John Whittle Appleyard, Wesleyan Missionary in South Africa, etc.* London, Wesleyan Missionary Society, 1881, p. 68–69.

I have been sadly inconvenienced for the want of a good compositor in the printing office at Mount Coke for some months past. I have advertised in the Frontier papers, but without being successful. I have been induced, therefore, to trouble you on this subject, as you may possibly have some printers either in the Bury or Sydney Street congregations who would not object to engage to take work at a Mission Station. I put an advertisement on the other side, which you would oblige me by having inserted twice in one or two of the Cape papers, as you may judge best. The salary I gave my last compositor, who was a respectable European, was £100 per annum. I should not like to go much beyond this amount, though to get a pious and orderly young man, I should not object to a small advance. He will have a private sleeping-room in connection with the office, but he will have to board himself.

I have no objection to respectable coloured persons, though I suppose their salaries are not so high as those of the European class. In that case, I should like to change my pressman and my bookbinder also, who are both a source of frequent annoyance to me, on account of their drinking habits and propensities. I fear, however, that one man will be as much as you can obtain at present, so I will say no more on this point further than if you hear there is any probability of my being able to obtain any such men, I should be glad if you would let me know. What I most need just now is a good compositor,—if he knows anything of press work as well, all the better.

When Appleyard had completed the translation of the whole Bible, he went to England to supervise the publishing of the work by the British and Foreign Bible Society, and was away until 15 February 1865, but continued to superintend the press on his return until his death in 1874. Then, as during Appleyard's stay in England, the Rev. W. Holford was put in charge. Circumstances had changed, and the press had served its purpose. It was therefore closed down shortly after it had once more been moved to Grahamstown in 1876. The Wesleyan Methodist Conference, however, in 1886 began to have doubts and considered what was best to do with such printing materials as were then still at Grahamstown and to investigate the probable cost of putting the old press into working order.

So much importance was placed on the translation and printing of the Xhosa Bible by Appleyard, that Mount Coke has been declared an historical monument by the Commission for the Preservation of Natural and Historical Monuments.

The assumption is that the continual moving of the press from one mission centre to another was necessary mainly to prevent its destruction during times of unrest, when stations were regularly burnt to the ground.

The 'Itinerancy of the Press', as Henry Cotton called it, is not an infrequent occurrence in South Africa, particularly in the field of mission work. W. R. Morrison reported[1] that there was an account in the Archives of the American Zulu Mission

1. Morrison, W. R. 'A Bibliographical Excursion' in *South African Libraries*, vol. 4, p. 36.

in Boston, U.S.A. to the effect that a handpress was moved from place to place on a wagon and that various tracts were printed in the vicinity of the Umlazi River in 1838. Here, at no great distance from present-day Durban, George Champion of the American Board of Commissioners for Foreign Missions built the first house of this group of missionaries on 22 February 1836 among the Zulu people of Natal. On 7 March of that year he started his first school, 'using the shade of a large tree for a school-room and the earth—the letters written in the sand—for an a-b-c book'.[1] Shortly after this date Champion was joined by Aldin Grout and Newton Adams, M.D., the other American missionaries assigned to Natal, and a little later, for a limited time, by Daniel Lindley after the failure of the mission to Mosega. Before 21 August 1837 the 'printing establishment', presented by General Champion at a cost of about five hundred dollars, and some paper were received from America and placed at Umlazi with Dr. Adams who had 'some knowledge of the art.'[2] Lindley and Adams tried their hand at printing and produced a few elementary books for the school.[3] When the troubles between the Boers and the Zulus broke out in Natal, the missionaries succeeded in saving their precious press and paper and actually took them on board ship when they sailed to Cape Town. In April 1838 the missionaries were corresponding about 'the deficiencies in their type', but by the end of 1840 more than 50,000 pages had been printed. Very little seems to have survived of these early publications. From 1841 onwards specimens of school books and religious publications are available. The earliest known Biblical translation seems to have been extracts from Genesis translated by Dr. Newton Adams (1806–1851) and printed at Umlazi in 1846. In 1847 Dr. Adams moved his mission to Amanzimtoti, and died on 16 September 1851 at the age of forty-five years, caused, it is said by overwork. His native name was 'the teacher with three coats' because he dressed differently when he practised medicine, when he preached, and when he printed! In 1881 there was still an echo of Dr. Adams, for in that year John Mavuma Nembula was sent to the U.S.A. to assist the typesetters with the printing of the Bible in Zulu. He was the grandson of one of Dr. Adam's first converts and grew up at Amanzimtoti. Nembula qualified as a medical doctor in Chicago in 1887, returned to South Africa, and practised medicine until his death in 1897.

1. Bliss, E. M., *ed. The Encyclopaedia of Missions: descriptive, historical, biographical, statistical, etc.* New York, Funk & Wagnall, 1891, vol. 2, p. 538.
2. Kotze, D. J., *ed. Letters of the American Missionaries, 1835–1838.* Cape Town, Van Riebeeck Society, 1950, p. 144, 145, 151 and 200.
3. Bliss, E. M., *ed. The Encyclopaedia of Missions: descriptive, historical, biographical, statistical, etc.* New York, Funk & Wagnall, 1891, vol. 2, p. 538.

Port Natal occurs in imprints on both secular and religious publications dated 1849 or 1850, but no records have so far been found of the missionary in charge of this press at this time.

Although Umbilo has not been recognized in an imprint, William Ireland, who arrived in 1849, noted that in 1850 John A. Butler came to take charge of the press at Umbilo, four miles from Durban.[1]

In the early part of 1859 a printing press was set up at Umsundisi, thirty miles from Durban. The Rev. Lewis Grout was in charge,[2] and in six months produced twice as much as had been done on the presses of the Colony during the seven previous years—that is, since the death of Newton Adams.[3] The earliest Umsundisi item listed is a Zulu translation by L. Grout of The Acts, which bears the date 1859.

Esidumbini, an American Board mission, some fifty miles north of Durban, figures in imprints in the eighteen sixties, though the station dates from 1849 when Josiah Tyler arrived. The journal, *Ikwezi* (Morning star), was issued here from 1861 to 1868 and, in 1865 a Zulu New Testament emanated from this press. Tyler's daughter noted that her father had 'an English printer' in charge at this time,[4] but his name has not been traced.

The American missionaries in Natal did much to further the Zulu translation of the Scriptures and to print their translations in Natal frequently using Zulu labour, for the Rev. William Ireland's Training School at Adams, Natal (formerly Amanzimtoti), established in 1865, included the teaching of printing in its curriculum.

Members of the Paris Evangelical Missionary Society landed in Cape Town from France in 1829, bringing with them a small printing press, type, and paper. After many vicissitudes, Samuel Rolland established Beerseba some miles from the present town of Smithfield in the Orange Free State. This was in 1835. The press was set up, and in 1841 some hymns were issued bearing the names of S. Rolland and H. Dyke and dated October. A few copies have survived of these single sheets which formed the basis of the Sesuto (or Sotho) hymn book. There were also a few tracts

1. Ireland, W. *Historical Sketch of the Zulu Mission in South Africa, etc.* Boston, American Board of Commissioners for Foreign Missions, [1865?], p. 18–19.
2. Gray, *Mrs.* M. W. (Tyler). *Stories of the early American Missionaries in South Africa.* No place, (P. C. Westwood, printer), [1934?], p. 54.
3. Bliss, E. M., *ed. The Encyclopaedia of Missions: descriptive, historical, biographical, statistical, etc.* New York, Funk & Wagnall, 1891, Vol. 2, p. 540.
4. Gray, *Mrs.* M. W. (Tyler). *Stories of the early American Missionaries in South Africa.* No place, (P. C. Westwood, printer), [1934?], p. 60.

and booklets, which, considering the extremely primitive conditions under which the missionaries were working, are a credit to them. A professional printer was soon requested from Paris.[1]

Du Plessis quotes Casalis[2] on how reluctant the Basuto were to learn to read, or, as they expressed it, 'make the paper speak', but once they had mastered the mechanics of reading, there was much excitement. This happened at Thaba Bosiu, where the chief, Moshesh, lived. At Morija the first ten scholars who had learned to read, 'received as a reward for their diligence, a copy each of the first book printed in the Sesuto language.'[3]

By 1845 the whole of the New Testament had been translated and was being printed at Beerseba, when the printer left. The thousand copies which were ready and included the Gospels and the Acts, were bound and issued. About four years later, the printing was completed with a separate title for the part added later. The printer who left was probably J. D. M. Ludorf, who, for a time, was a Wesleyan missionary. A journal, *Mobeleli oa litaba*, was printed at Beerseba from 8 October 1841 to May 1846. It contained extracts from the Bible, and had a woodcut of a press with a motto meaning 'A press is a well which pours forth knowledge on the earth'. The source of this cut has not been traced, but it is almost certainly not to have been of local manufacture. Apart from vignettes received in the ordinary way as part of a printer's stock in trade, it is on record that Mission headquarters in Europe sent cuts to South African and other mission presses, as is clear from the *Report* of the Centenary Conference on Foreign Missions held in London in 1888, when the representative of the London Missionary Society paid tribute to the Tract Society for this kind of assistance.[4] Woodcuts had been used in 1840–1841 at Kuruman, as is evident from Item 306 in Bleek's catalogue. One of these days it may be possible to determine in which overseas publications the cuts used by South African mission presses first appeared.

When war broke out in 1858, the French missionaries fled from Beerseba, taking their press and type with them. The press is next heard of at Bethesda, which was founded in 1843 on the northern bank of the Orange River. Here school songs were

1. 'Basutoland Printing Works', etc. reprinted from *R & L News*, the house organ of Reunert and Lenz in *Press News*, January 1952, p. 14.
2. Casalis, E. *The Basutos; or, Twenty-three Years in South Africa.* London, James Nisbet, 1861, p. 82.
3. Du Plessis, J. *A History of Christian Missions in South Africa;* facsimile reprint [of the 1911 edition]. Cape Town, C. Struik, 1965, p. 198.
4. *Centenary Conference on Foreign Missions*, London, 1888. *Report* ... ed. by James Johnstone, *etc.* London, James Nisbet, 1888, vol. 1, p. 449.

printed in 1866. The press was transferred to Morija in 1874,[1] and so was that from Masitisi in 1875, where D. F. Ellenberger had printed the Book of Genesis and Psalms in Sotho in 1872.

Morija had been established in 1834, and there in 1860 Adolphe Mabille set up the press he had brought with him in 1858. He issued tracts at Morija in 1860, and his *Arithmetic* is dated 1871. By 1876 he had printed over a million pages in the year, and the next year his trained printers numbered ten. He turned out school books, readers, geography books as well as religious matter, working not only for the Mission but also for the Government. Among other things he introduced the Tonic Sol-Fa notation among the Basuto and, with permission from John Curwen, the inventor of this notation, printed the first hymn book in Sotho with this notation in 1877, having first imported the required type.[2]

Major Tylden tells of the manner in which the Morija Mission Printing Press lost the Government Printing contract: On 17 March 1880 a Disarmament Proclamation was sent to Mabille for translation into Sotho and printing, but as the missionary disapproved of the date set for disarmament, he refused either to translate or print the proclamation. Consequently Morija lost the Government printing contract, and an unpleasant correspondence followed between the Government and the missionaries.[3] But nevertheless Mabille, who had no grant for the press, made it pay for itself, printing in thirty different languages on all kinds of subjects for a variety of customers ranging from individuals and missionary societies to the Government.

By 1882 he had collected approximately £3,000 for a new press, which unfortunately arrived at Morija in a damaged state and without diagrams. Mabille, with the help of the mission blacksmith and the head of the Industrial School, put the press into working order. He taught the Basuto to print, and soon had a number of journeymen and apprentices at work.

In 1894 Alfred Casalis took charge of the press, which continues to produce good work. Mr. J. Zurcher, at the time manager of the Morija Printing Works, in response to a request for information about any surviving printing plant of historic interest replied c. 1958 that there still was an old cropper dating back to about 1880 that had been used from the time of the Rev. Adolphe Mabille right up until about 1950. When Mr. Zurcher arrived in 1920, there was scattered bits of 'the old cast iron hand press' left, but there was not enough to reconstruct it.

1. Smith, E. W. *The Mabilles of Basutoland*. London, Hodder & Stoughton, 1939, p. 223.
2. Dieterlen, H. *Adolphe Mabille Missionnaire, etc.* Paris, Société des Missions évangéliques; 1898, p. 170–171.
3. Tylden, G. *The Rise of the Basuto*. Cape Town, Juta, 1950, p. 140.

The Morija Mission Press probably has been in continuous production longer than any other mission press in Southern Africa.

The Anglicans were late in starting mission work in South Africa, and the earliest reference to a mission press mentions to that of Bishop Colenso at Bishopstowe near Pietermaritzburg under its African name of Ekukanyeni. The press was in operation from about the year 1858 and issued books of hymns, prayers, and translations of various books of the Old Testament in 1859. It is on record that eighteen books prepared by the Bishop for the use of missionary students were largely printed by a Zulu. Apparently he managed the press in the Bishop's absence overseas without supervision, correcting the sheets with the greatest accuracy and sending the proofs regularly once a month to England.[1] At one stage this press kept four good printers occupied.

In 1858 Bishop Gray, to whose enthusiasm the inception of mission work in South Africa by the Church of England was due, started a college for the sons of native chiefs at Bishopscourt, Cape Town. Two years later the institution was moved to the estate of Zonnebloem, in the neighbourhood of Cape Town, and at some unspecified date, a press was installed there, and *Prayers and Forms to be learnt by heart* in English and Xhosa in parallel columns was printed at Zonnebloem in the early days. Between 1854 and 1857 four stations, named after the evangelists, were established in Kaffraria.

St. Mathew's Press at Keiskamma Hoek is reported as the press from which tracts in Xhosa emanated in 1861 and an almanac in 1862,[2] and a bilingual letter-writer and conversations both edited by W. Greenstock are noted under 1865 in Th. Hahn's *Index of the Grey Collection*.[3] The Rev. W Greenstock (1859–1870) was the founder. Some ten years later the press was removed by the Rev. A. J. Newton to the mission at Gwatyu to supplement the press already in operation. In 1878 Gwatyu was destroyed, and Newton opened a new press at Lanti on the Indwe River, and named it St. Peter's-on-Indwe. Gwatyu, Lanti and St. Peter's-on-Indwe all occur in imprints between 1869 and 1894.

In 1887 a new start was made at St. Matthew's by the Rev. C. Taberer, and in

1. Cox, *Sir* George W. *The Life of John William Colenso, D. D., Bishop of Natal.* London, W. Ridgway, 1888, vol. 1, p. 84.
2. Pascoe, C. F. *Two hundred Years of the S.P.G.: an historical account of the Society for the Propagation of the Gospel in Foreign Parts, 1701–1900, etc.* London, The Society, 1901, p. 803.
3. Hahn, Th. *An Index of the Grey Collection in the South African Public Library*, Cape Town, Saul Solomon, 1884, p. 122–123.

1896 the whole plant at St. Peter's was transferred to St. Matthew's. The Rev. C. J. Wyche enlarged the scope of the press during the later years of the century.[1]

Between 1871 and 1875 from St. John's Mission Press various Books of the Old Testament and school readers in Xhosa were issued, but no details of the history of the press have been found.

The Rev. H. T. Waters worked at St. Mark's, and Hahn[2] lists various quarterly reports, between 30 June 1877 to 30 September 1880, with the imprint 'St. Mark's Mission, Transkei', but again no records relating to the work of this press have been traced.

Fortunately a little more is known of the printing press operated in Natal by the Anglican Bishop Henry Callaway. Springvale in Southern Natal was a station of the 'Maritzburg Mission Association for the Diocese of Natal' and the press was established after June 1865, presumably the one recorded as given to Dr. Callaway by a friend in England.[3] The superior quality of the work done by this press is no doubt due to the 'first-rate English printer engaged to superintend the native training'.[4] He was John A. Blair who recorded that the press was set up in the 'verandah-rooms of the school-church, next to the doctor's study'. Here Blair printed not only religious works but also Dr. Callaway's two very important studies, *Nursery Tales, Traditions and Histories of the Zulus* (also with a Zulu title) in 1866–1868, and *The Religious System of the Amazulu* in 1869–1870.

When Dr. Callaway became bishop, John Blair moved the press to a 'more commodious building' at Highflats, not very far from Springvale. Here he printed the Bishop's Zulu translation of the four Gospels in 1877. Later Blair joined the Bishop at Umtata, but details of the work done there have not been found.

Two other places in Natal are recorded as having printing presses belonging to the Church of England. A Zulu prayer book, revised by Bishop Mackenzie with the assistance of other missionaries, was printed at Isandhlwana in 1885, but earlier than this a single sheet in English, Zulu, and Sotho, the 'Our Father', was printed at Isandhlwana and bears the legend 'First attempt with the Mission Press, Isandhlwana

1. Bulwer, C. E. E. 'Xhosa Language and Literature: the contribution of the Church of the Province of S.A.' in *South African Outlook*, March, 1957, p. 44–45.
2. Hahn, Th. *An Index of the Grey Collection in the South African Public Library*. Cape Town, Saul Solomon, 1884, p. 232–233.
3. Darlow, T. H. and H. F. Moule. *Historical Catalogue of the Printed Editions of Holy Scripture in the Library of the British and Foreign Bible Society*. London, Bible House, 1903–1911, p. 1716.
4. Benham, M. S. *Henry Callaway, M.D., D.D., first Bishop for Kaffraria: his Life-history and Work: a Memoir, etc.* London, Macmillan, 1896, p. 164, 166.

Single sheet giving the Lord's Prayer in English, Zulu, and Sotho, printed by the Anglican mission press Isandhlwana (Natal), obviously before *Bishop Mackenzie's Zulu prayer book of 1885, its earliest dated publicatic (Approximately natural size.) Original in the Africana Museum, Johannesbu*

ENGLISH.

OUR FATHER which art in heaven, Hallowed be thy name. Thy kingdom come. Thy will be done in earth as it is in heaven. Give us this day our daily bread. And forgive us our trespasses, as we forgive them that trespass against us. And lead us not into temptation, But deliver us from evil. For thine is the kingdom, the power, and the glory, for ever and ever. Amen.

ZULU.

BABA WETU osezulwini, Malahlukaniswe igama lako. Mauze umbuso wako. Mayenziwe intando yako emhlabeni njenga sezulwini. Sipe namuhla ukudhla kwetu kwanamuhla. Sitetelele izono zetu, njengokuba nati sibatetelele abasonayo. Ungasiyisi ekulingweni; kodwa sikulule kwokubi. Ngokuba umbuso ungowako, namandhla, nobukosi, kuze kube pakade. Amen.

SESUTO.

NTAT 'A RONA a magodimong, Lebitso la gao le galalele. 'Muso oa gao o tlle. Thato ea gao e etsoe lefatseng, jualeka legodimong. U re fe *k*ajeno bogobe ba rona ba tsatsi le leng le le leng. U re leselle melato ea rona, jualeka ha re lesella ba re sitetsoeng. 'Me U se *k*e ua re isa molekong: empa U re loele bobeng. Gobane 'muso *k*e oa gao, le matla, le *k*hanya, *k*a go sa eeng *k*ae. Amen.

First attempt with the Mission Press,
Isandhlwana.

A. M. D. G.

A.M.D.G.', but unfortunately no date. The press was transferred from Isandhlwana to Eshowe in the 'nineties where Zulu hymns (1896) and a catechism in Zulu (1898) were printed.

It is believed that this press is the one which was used by the Church of England at Thaba 'Nchu and Bloemfontein in the Orange Free State. Although the Wesleyans had a mission and a press at this place, the Anglicans also started at Thaba 'Nchu in 1865. William Crisp[1] states that a small press was bought with the aid of F. W. Doxat in 1867. Before Easter 1876 Thaba 'Nchu received a press capable of carrying a double demy and also a fair amount of type as a gift from the Society for Promoting Christian Knowledge. When Crisp left Thaba 'Nchu, the press was removed to the Theological College in Bloemfontein, probably about 1886. Hymns, prayers, and spelling books were issued at Thaba 'Nchu before the new press was received, and it is on record that the printers experienced considerable difficulties because they had so little type and such a small press. As the press had to be self-supporting, there was very little profit even about 1870, when an edition of 600 Serolong (a dialect of Tswana) spelling books was sold at threepence each. The printer stated that the trifle paid for the book barely covered the cost of the paper, and also drew attention to the cost of carriage. The Serolong Prayer Book printed in 1875 was published in an edition of 1,000 copies and was bound in strong boards covered with black American cloth[2]—a commonly used material for book covers of an inexpensive kind right up to the first years of this century.

From the middle of the last century various missionaries belonging to the Lutheran Church were responsible for printing in Southern Africa, but, generally speaking they relied to a great extent on sending their manuscripts overseas for printing. In passing it should be noted that one of the earliest works ever printed in South-West Africa is a Lutheran catechism translated into Nama-Hottentot and printed by the Rhenish missionary, the Rev. H. Kleinschmidt of Rhehoboth, a station near Walvis Bay. This seventeen-page pamphlet was ready in 1855,[3] and the imprint reads Scheppmannsdorf.

In the Transvaal Merensky of the Berlin Mission established a station in 1864 north-east of Pretoria, and south-east of Lydenburg, which he named Botshabelo

1. Crisp, W. *Some Account of the Diocese of Bloemfontein in the Province of South Africa from 1863 to 1894.* Oxford, James Parker, 1895, p. 49, 51, 52.

2. *Quarterly Paper of the Bloemfontein Mission*, January 1871, p. 19 and October 1875, p. 24.

3. Bleek, W. H. I. *The Library of ... Sir George Grey: philology: v. I, pt. I: South Africa.* London, Trübner, 1858, Item 12.

or city of refuge, to which he encouraged people to come who had fallen foul of Sekukuni the chief of the Pedi. From about 1878 printing and book-binding departments were in operation here.

The Lutheran Church of Sweden established a mission in the Natal town of Dundee, c. 1889, and its Ebenezer Press has been responsible for a supply of missionary literature.

The Moravians who were the first of all the Protestant societies to send missionaries to South Africa, were also, on the whole, among the most successful. Yet, the first reference to a printing press at their station Genadendal in the Western Cape Province, occurs in 1859, when a Dutch reader by P. Hallbeck was issued; but after that date a considerable number of publications in Dutch and in some African languages, as well as mission journals appeared.

The Roman Catholic Church, according to Du Plessis, has a different approach to mission work from that of the Protestant churches,[1] but nevertheless it is possible to include the work done at the Trappist monastery of Mariannhill, near Pinetown, Natal, since 1883,[2] under mission presses. Publications in languages as diverse as Polish and Zulu have emanated from this press, and during the first year of the monastery, a vernacular catechism, some broadsides in English and German among which were some hymns.[3]

To most of the missionaries printing was simply a means to an end, and consequently details of the press or type they used are rarely to be found in an account of a missionary's life and work.

Although only a fraction of the products of the mission presses has been enumerated in this survey and many of the presses and even the names of missionary societies active at the time have been omitted either through ignorance of their existence or because none of their products have survived, it is nevertheless hoped that some indication has been given of the important part played by mission presses in the spread of printing in Southern Africa during the nineteenth century. It is also hoped that some idea has been given of the difficulties under which these presses operated thousands of miles away from the source of supply of everything from the press and the type to the paper and the printer. One can but admire the industry, patience, resourcefulness, and courage of the missionary printer.

1. Du Plessis, J. *A History of Christian Missions in South Africa;* facsimile reprint [of the 1911 edition]. Cape Town, C. Struik, 1965, p. 368. 2. Davies, H. *Great South African Christians.* Cape Town, O.U.P., 1951, p. 89. 3. *Das Trappisten-Missionskloster Mariannhill; oder, Bilder aus dem afrikanischen Missionsleben, etc.* Freiburg im Breisgau, Herdersche Verlagshandlung, 1907, p. 10.

The composing room (top) and bindery (bottom) of the (originally German) Trappist monastery at Mariann (Natal), round the turn of the century. From: Das Trappisten-Missionskloster Mariannhill, *Freiburg/Br. 1*

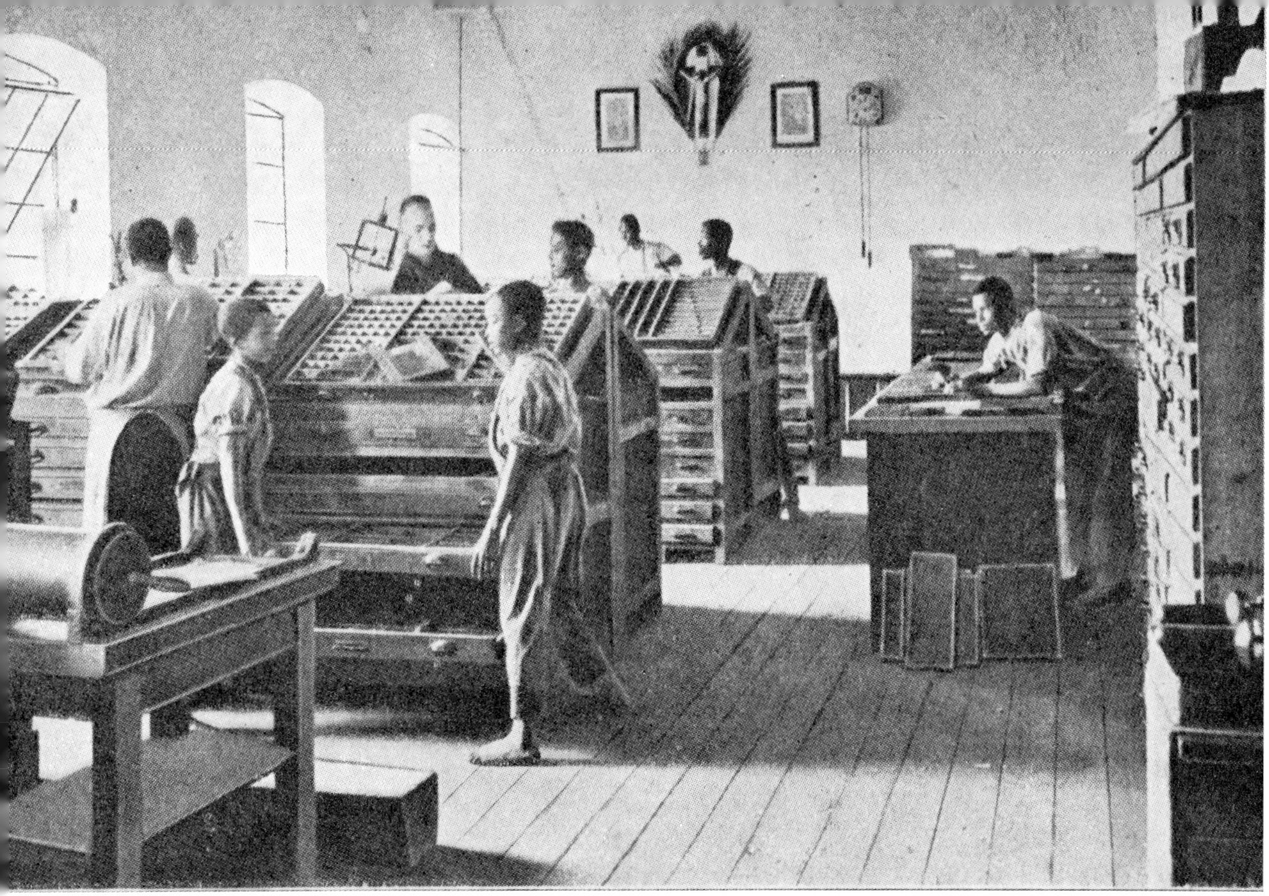

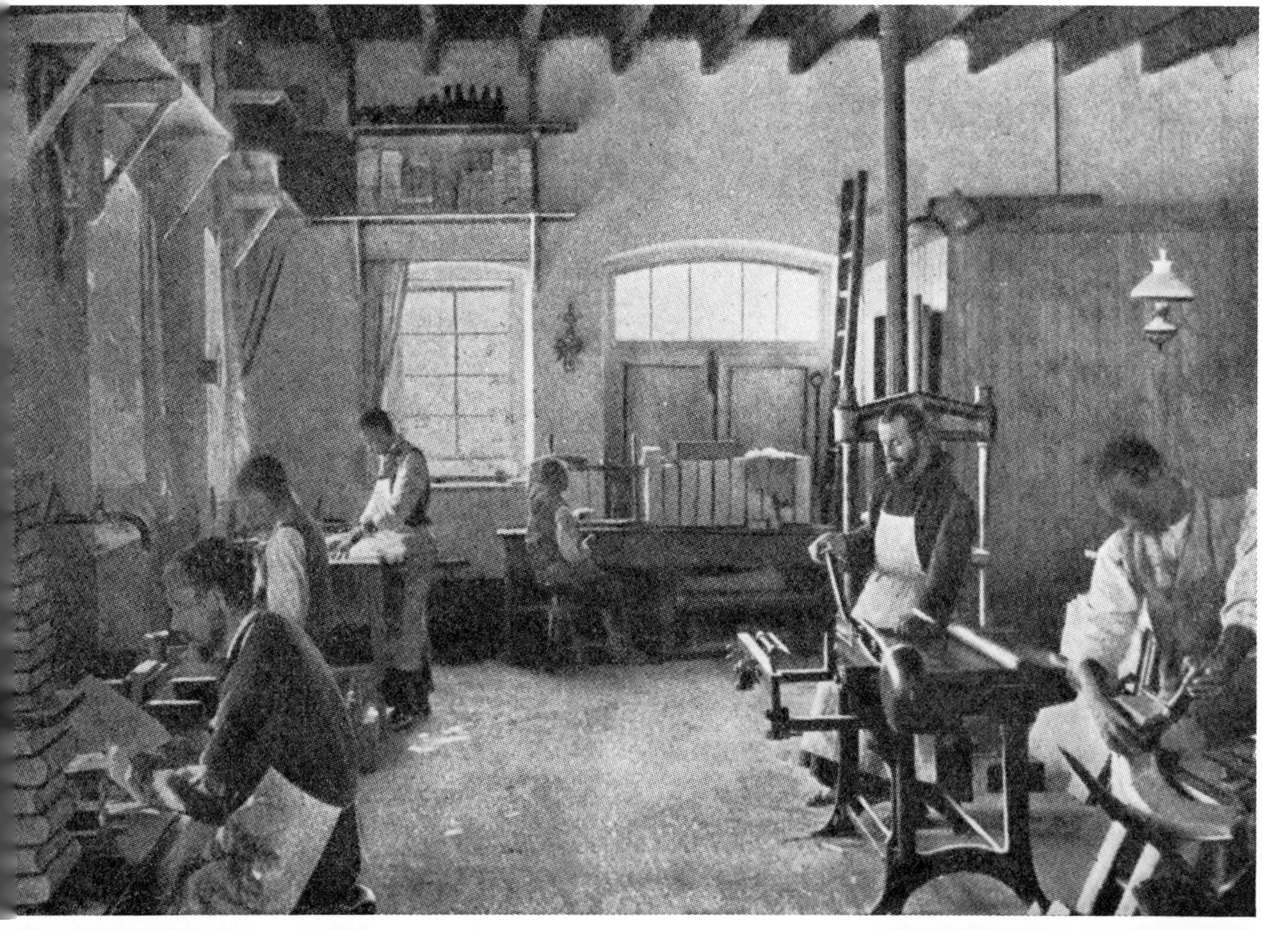

Country Presses in the Cape Colony

After Greig, Pringle and Fairbairn had succeeded in obtaining a free press for Cape Town, various independent printers established themselves, and there was a substantial increase in the number of journals and newspapers published in the town. But outside of Cape Town, except for mission presses, printing spread slowly.

The earliest place outside Cape Town to have a secular press was Graaff Reinet. Dr. Laidler listed a form concerning the right to water for irrigation at Graaff Reinet, which J. G. Gubbins of Ottoshoop, Tvl., owned c. 1935. Dr. Laidler dated it 18 (27).[1] *South Africa in Print*, the catalogue of a special exhibition of books etc. in the South African Public Library, Cape Town in March/April 1952 includes *Instructions for the Overseer and Director of Dams, Canals, Sluices and Sluice-houses in the Town of Graaff-Reinet.* A. Stockenstrom. District Press. 2 September 1822[2]. In the Wagner collection of Africana now owned by the Department of Education, Arts and Science and housed in Pretoria is an identical specimen. Meurant[3] tells of an amateur printer, P. C. Wahlstrand, who 'was employed in printing Government forms for the use of the public offices, the salary of the printer amounting to more than the 'forms' were worth'. Meurant also states that the old-style wooden press Wahlstrand was using was the identical press the 1820 British Settlers, Robert Godlonton and Thomas Stringfellow, had brought with them, but been forbidden to take to the Eastern Province by the Cape authorities. But there must have been

1. Laidler, P. W. *The Pre-Victorian Products of the Cape Press, 1796–1837:* being a chronological bibliography with annotations of all civil products of the Cape Press.
2. *South Africa in Print: Catalogue of an Exhibition of Books, Atlases and Maps held in the South African Library, Cape Town, 1 March till 5 April 1952 in Commemoration of the arrival of Jan van Riebeeck at the Cape 6 April 1652.* Cape Town, Book Exhibition Committee Van Riebeeck Festival, 1952, p. 166, No. 38.
3. Meurant, L. H. *Sixty Years Ago; or, Reminiscences of the Struggle for Freedom of the Press in South Africa, and the Establishment of the first Newspaper in the Eastern Province, etc.* Cape Town, Saul Solomon, 1885, p. 77.

yet an earlier press at Graaff Reinet, for *South Africa in Print* also includes *Publicatie-regulatien omtrent de Straten en Waterleiding*. A. Stockenstrom. Districts Drukkery. 8 July 1817. It is believed that a form emanating from the Districts Drukkery, Graaff Reinet, exists which bears the date '8 Meij 1817'. It is said to have the 'three plumes' coat of arms with the motto 'Ich dien'. Neither of the last two forms could have been printed on the so-called 'Settlers' press', which only arrived in 1820. Nothing seems to be known of the printer, who is listed in the *Cape Almanac* of 1825 as 'Wahlstrand, P. C., District printer, Graaff Reinet', and must still have been so employed in 1828 at the time of Meurant's visit to Graaff Reinet.

When the Settlers' press was put up for auction at Graaff Reinet in 1829, Meurant bought it, and took press and plant to Grahamstown, where he started a printing works in September 1830 and in the same year published the first book issued in Grahamstown, *An[!] Eulogy on Dr. Alexander Cowie and Mr. Benjamin Green who lost their Lives, on their Return from Delagoa Bay to Graham's Town*, by T. P. Adams.

This press was bought from a staff member of the King's Printing Office in London by Dr. Edward Roberts, when he came to South Africa with the 1820 Settlers. The intention was that it should be used in South Africa by Robert Godlonton assisted by Stringfellow and Mollett to produce a newspaper to be sent to the Settlers' families in England. But this was not to be in 1820[1] as the Government took possession of the press, and according to information supplied to Meurant by P. C. Wahlstrand and the Civil commissioner of Graaff Reinet in 1828–29, the confiscated press was the one sold to Meurant. Not long after it arrived in Grahamstown, Meurant started the first newspaper issued outside Cape Town, the influential *Grahamstown Journal*, of which the first issue was published on 30 December 1831. It was a half sheet double crown, and Meurant had no skilled printers to assist him. He had no 'composition' rollers or balls and he was editor, printer, publisher, and proprietor, to start with. He had some assistance from Lt. T. C. White, until his death in the War of 1834–35, and then from W. Beddy, formerly of *The Colonist*, Cape Town. In the beginning of 1834 Robert Godlonton became the editor, and in July 1834 Meurant and Godlonton became partners for a period of five years. When this period expired, Meurant in July 1839 sold his share to Godlonton, who in this manner became the owner of the press which he had hoped to use in 1820. Meurant

1. Campbell, C. T. *British South Africa: a History of the Colony of the Cape of Good Hope from its Conquest 1795 to the Settlement of Albany by the British Emigration of 1819, etc.* London, John Haddon, 1897, p. 115.

on his own and in partnership with Godlonton and later with Franklin, printed various interesting and important publications, such as the first Wesleyan Catechism in Xhosa in 1832; and in 1837, probably the first Dutch religious pamphlet, *Een Kort Verhaal van den Vader*, etc. (a short story by the father about the life and death of his two daughters) issued outside Cape Town. In 1840 Meurant was associated with the *Cape Frontier Times*, followed by *Het Kaapsche Grensblad* in 1844, and *The Cradock News* as well as the *Cradocksche Nieuwsblad* in c. 1858 and 1861. In the last two named, Meurant's famous dialogues in Afrikaans were first published. In 1861 they were issued as a separate publication called *Zamenspraak tusschen Klaas Waarzegger en Jan Twyfelaar*, etc. and printed by J. S. Bold in Cradock. Meurant is therefore generally considered as the author of the first book written in Afrikaans, and believed to have stopped printing himself when he left Grahamstown in 1853. He became a magistrate, and later a member of the old Cape House. He was born in Cape Town in June 1811, and died in Riversdale in 1893, having taken an active part in printing and journalism from the time he was apprenticed to Greig in Cape Town until the end of his life.

In South Africa throughout the nineteenth century almost every newspaper printer was also the jobbing printer for the area in which he was established, and the history of printing is therefore very closely bound up with the history of the press. It is, consequently, the date of the establishment of the first newspaper in a particular town that is in most cases the date when printing was first practised in the place.

The South African Commercial Advertiser of 24 May 1845 welcomed *The Eastern Province Herald*, of which the first number appeared in Port Elizabeth on 7 May 1845, in the following words:

> Among the symptoms of a growing community, the extension of Printing, if it be gradual, is one of the most certain. To support a Press a considerable mass of educated population is required, and that implies wealth, and wealth implies the labor of numbers. In 1832 there was but one Press in the Colony, and it was the Government Press. There are now (1845) Ten Newspapers —the tenth having just opened its batteries at Port Elizabeth, Algoa Bay, under the name of the 'EASTERN PROVINCE HERALD.'

The publication of this newspaper was announced in a pamphlet which appeared on 2 April 1845 in which the public were told to expect the new paper sometime in May of that year. It started in Titterton Buildings in Titterton Lane off Main Street, Port Elizabeth, as a weekly, then became a tri-weekly, and on 31 January 1898, daily.

The *Eastern Province Herald* still exists, and is now the second oldest paper in South Africa.

The first printer-publisher of this paper was John Ross Philip, a son of Dr. John Philip of the London Missionary Society. Until early in 1845 J. R. Philip[1] was the third partner in the Cape Town firm of Richert, Pike and Philip, but at that time John Paterson persuaded him to come to Port Elizabeth to start the *Eastern Province Herald*. Philip established *Port Elizabeth Mercury* on 5 March 1850. He died on 18 July 1898 at the age of eighty-two.

The driving force in Port Elizabeth was John Paterson, a Scottish schoolmaster, who later became the owner of the paper, a member of the Legislative Assembly, and a businessman. Paterson imported printing materials himself and started *The Eastern Province News* in 1849. By arrangement, the title of *The Eastern Province News* was changed to *Eastern Province Herald*. In October 1857 George Impey and others purchased the plant, and E. H. Walton joined in 1878.[2]

Two books published in 1852 under John Paterson's imprint and using the same press as the *Eastern Province Herald*, seem to be the earliest books printed in Port Elizabeth. They are M. B. Hudson's poem, *A Feature in South African Frontier Life*, and *A Manual of the Geography of British South Africa*, by John Gibson.

Fort Beaufort appears to be the next place at which a press was in operation, but as the only item traced has no printer's name, it is possible that it was printed by a mission press in the area. However it may be, a proclamation issued by the Government in Xhosa concerning the laws affecting the Fingo *(Imiteto ka Government Kubo bonke abantu abahleliyo emizini yamam Fengu)* is listed by Bleek, as having been published in 1853.[3] There must have been considerable activity in the vicinity of Fort Beaufort in the 'forties and 'fifties, for here it was that Alfred Essex (1818–90) found work as the manager of the London Missionary Society's printing press, before going to start the *Graaff Reinet Herald* on 25 August 1852, where he was joined in 1853 by his brother-in-law, William Henry Rabone (1824–1902). The latter had worked for E. C. Osborne in Birmingham and in London for the firm of Bradbury and Evans (where *Punch* and the works of Dickens were printed), and later in the United States, and was probably the most experienced printer of his

1. Redgrave, J. J. *Port Elizabeth in Bygone Days*. Wynberg, Rustica Press, printer, 1947, p. 116 *and* ffolliott, P. & E. L. H. Croft. *One Titan at a Time, etc.* Cape Town, Howard Timmins, (1960), p. 77–84.
2. *Eastern Province Herald*, 27 June 1953.
3. Bleek, W. H. I. *The Library of ... Sir George Grey: philology: vol. I, pt. I; South Africa*. London, Trubner, 1858, p. 81, No. 160.

time in the Cape Colony. Some of the experiences of these two printers in the Graaff Reinet area are told in their own letters in *Records of a Pioneer Family* (issued by C. Struik of Cape Town in 1966). On 14 February 1948, the editor of these *Records*, Mr. A. Rabone, personally stated that Alfred Essex bought the press and type used for *Sam Sly's African Journal* from the owner W. L. Sammons, and took them to Graaff Reinet for the *Graaff Reinet Herald*. In 1884 all the *Herald* machinery was sold to the *Richmond Era*, which had been established on 24 September 1870.

Unfortunately no printer's name appears on F. A. du Toit's *Kommandant der Beaufort Burgermagt: nuwe Aantekeningen van de Werkelijke Dienst*, recorded as having been printed at Grootfontein in 1846, by *South Africa in Print*.[1] The *Umtata Occasional Register*, again without printer's name, is listed under 1849 by *South Africa in Print*[2] which gives the same year as the beginnings of a commercial press in King William's Town, but so far no surviving piece of printing from this town bears as early a date. *The Cradock Dispatch*, which started in November 1850, and only survived until 5 December 1850, is the earliest known printing in the town of Cradock. O. W. Jeffrey is named as associated with it, but nothing is known about him, and he may not have been a printer. W. R. Morrison[3] states that printing first occurred in East London in 1850, but Dr. Laidler questioned this, and suggested c. 1865;[4] unfortunately neither authority recorded either printer or item.

A pioneer printer of King William's Town and East London was Solomon E. Rowles, an 1820 Settler who was born in Stroud, Gloucestershire, in 1818. He served his apprenticeship with Meurant and Franklin in Grahamstown, and later worked for Godlonton and White on the *Grahamstown Journal*, who sent him to King William's Town, where he started *The King William's Town Gazette* in 1855. In 1866 he established *The Kaffrarian Watchman* in King William's Town, and on 24 June 1872 he advertised that *The East London Daily Dispatch and Shipping and Mercantile Gazette* would soon start. The first number appeared on 10 September 1872 in East London. It was edited and printed by William Massey-Hicks, who erected his press in the kitchen of a house. The cottage next door was soon taken over.

1. *South Africa in Print: Catalogue of en Exhibition of Books, Atlases and Maps held in the South African Library, Cape Town, 1 March till 5 April 1952 in Commemoration of the arrival of Jan van Riebeeck at the Cape 6 April 1652*. Cape Town, Book Exhibition Committee Van Riebeeck Festival, 1952, p. 167, No. 43.
2. *Ibidem*, p. 167, No. 44.
3. Morrison, W. R. *A Brief History of South African Printing ... and Catalogue of Exhibition of Early South African Printing*. [Johannesburg?], no pub., [1934?], p. 12.
4. *South African Libraries*, vol. 6, p. 69 n.

W. A. Richards & Co. purchased the paper from Rowles, who died in King William's Town in October 1880.[1] The newspaper still exists as *The Daily Dispatch*. The earliest publications bearing the name of S. E. Rowles so far traced are a Xhosa life of Christ printed for the Berlin Mission in 1842, a Xhosa version of Dr. Watts' catechism dated 1853, and various tracts issued about this time.

Burghersdorp had its *Albert Times and Aliwal North Advertiser* in January 1855, printed by John Collins Eckley, formerly of Cape Town and employed by George Greig. Colesberg, Queenstown, and Swellendam all began printing in 1859. W. S. Giddy was printing in Colesberg, while David Solomon Barrable started *The Queenstown Free Press* in January 1859 and managed it for forty years. He was born on 9 May 1835 in Purfleet, Essex, and came to South Africa in 1847. He was trained on the *Grahamstown Journal* and, as so many other nineteenth-century printers, transported his plant by ox wagon to Queenstown in 1858.[2] H. H. Dugmore's *The American Preacher* was issued in 1866 with Barrable's imprint. On 5 October 1859 Pike and Byles started the *Overberg Courant* in Swellendam. It was a bilingual weekly and the first newspaper to be issued in the Western Province beyond the Hottentot's Holland Mountains—hence the name Overberg for the area, meaning beyond the mountains. The newspaper lasted until 10 May 1865. On 17 May a spark from a baker's oven started a fire in Swellendam, and forty buildings, including that which housed the press, were gutted.[3] The firm issued various religious and other publications of which eight are known to have survived and are listed by Dr. Burrows.[4] The partners in the firm were George James Pike and John Byles, who are listed in the *Cape Town Directory* of 1867 as working at 44 St. George's Street in Cape Town. One of their employees at Swellendam was J. P. Borrius.[5]

In 1862 Keiskamma Hoek followed with the *North Lincoln Sphinx* a periodical printed for private circulation among members of the Tenth Regiment; Uitenhage with *The Times* came in 1864, and in the same year on 1 December the *George*

1. Burton, A. W. Typescript on the Press on the Border, 5 August 1958, p. 4–6. [Unpublished].
2. *Anglo-African Who's who*, 1910, p. 20.
3. Burrows, E. H. *Overberg Outspan: a Chronicle of People and Places in the South Western Districts of the Cape, etc.* Cape Town, Maskew Miller, (1952), p. 81–82.
4. *Ibidem*, p. 302.
5. Nienaber, P. J. *Afrikaanse Biografiese Woordeboek.* Johannesburg, L. & S. Boek- en Kunssentrum, 1947, vol. 1, p. 37–38.

Advertiser began in George, while Beaufort West had its *Beaufort Courier* on 1 October 1869.[1]

By this time diamonds had been discovered in the vicinity of present-day Kimberley, and life in South Africa changed completely. In 1870 printing was started at Pniel on the Vaal River, opposite what is today known as Barkly West. *South Africa in Print* lists a newspaper *Diamond Field* as published on 13 October 1870, and another, *Diamond News* on 16 October 1870. The imprint of the last item reads 'Richards, Glanville & Co., Pniel, Vaal River.'[2] This venture was sponsored by the *Grahamstown Journal*. When diamonds were also discovered some distance away from the river diggings, the last paper was transferred to Dorstfontein, to be near the mines at Dutoitspan, Bultfontein, Colesberg Kopje and New Rush (the later Kimberley), in September 1871.

H. M. Guest (born in 1854) in March 1925 told the story of the Grahamstown party to *The South African Printer and Stationer* (p. 115–116) as follows:

> It was in 1870, he writes, that Messrs. Richards, Glanville & Co., Grahamstown, attracted by the movement of so many people towards the Vaal, decided to extend their business in that direction. Their preparations were crude and meagre, but sufficient for the purpose. The *Journal* office was denuded of its very oldest type and other simple but most necessary plant, and an old hand-press known in the trade as a double-demy Albion was dragged from its obscurity. A frame-house about 12 ft. by 24 ft. was constructed and packed, paper and other necessary articles collected, and food, consisting of meal, coffee, sugar, bacon, etc., sufficient to supply the party for six months, was loaded up on two wagons, each of which had a small tent to provide sleeping accommodation.
>
> The party consisted of three diggers and three printers, Mr. Guest among the latter. Mr. T. B. Glanville was head of the party and the editor of the projected journal.
>
> The wagons set out on their long trek over tracts of country hardly marked by traffic and sluits primitive and dangerous. At length Cradock was reached, the party by this time having settled down to the lumbering motion of the wagons and the temporary life they had entered. They collected fuel, made the fires, yelled at the oxen, carried water from adjacent dams or streams, greased the wheels, etc. Colesberg—then an irregular line of houses and huts—was passed. The crossing of the Orange River was effected with some little difficulty, the drift in the middle being deep enough to compel the oxen to swim. At Phillipolis [sic] a halt was made to discover the track to be followed. The succeeding experiences are best told by Mr. Guest's own words:—

1. *South Africa in Print: Catalogue of an Exhibition of Books, Atlases and Maps held in the South African Library, Cape Town, 1 March till 5 April 1952 in Commemoration of the arrival of Jan van Riebeeck at the Cape 6 April 1652.* Cape Town, Book Exhibition Committee Van Riebeeck Festival, 1952, p. 169, No. 58.

2. *South African Libraries*, Vol. 6, p. 70 n.

'The traffic on the road to the Diamond Fields was of a varied, curious and interesting nature. Numbers of men were seen trudging along on foot, with billy, food and blankets and other necessaries, singly, in couples, or in larger parties. Two men were passed trundling a wheelbarrow bearing their goods and chattels. Parties of men had clubbed together and secured a Scotch cart and one or two pair of oxen, which they traded for blankets and food, and walked themselves. Water was very scarce along the journey, and especially the pedestrians must have suffered severely from this. Our own party was thirty-six hours without water prior to reaching the Riet River.

'There the oxen failed to observe the mud lying between themselves and the river when they went down to drink, and we found a number with only their heads visible. Various means of recovery were suggested. One man tried to wade in to help them, but he only sank up to his neck and escaped suffocation by hanging on to the bullock's horns. There was some difficulty in rescuing him.

'All other schemes failing, reins were fastened round the unfortunate animals' horns, and these were attached to a trek chain lengthened sufficiently to reach the top of the bank running parallel with the river. Six oxen were attached, and the word to trek was given, accompanied by a persuasive sjambok. A mighty pull, which threatened to pull off the head of the submerged animal, was brought into play, and the poor beast drawn from the sticky mess. The animal was then lead, pushed, and carried up a path to the higher ground. The rescued animals were so exhausted that they were left out all night to recover. Only one succumbed to the effects of submersion.'

In this way did the pioneers of present-day journalism lay the modest foundations of the now efficient newspaper services on the Diamond Fields, Johannesburg, Barberton, and other remoter parts of South Africa, and among these pioneers Grahamstown furnished the greater number.

The plant of the *Diamond News* was sold to John E. Radford, who changed the name to *The Diamond Fields Advertiser*. This was in 1878.

For obvious reasons, the places within easy reach of Cape Town were very late in getting printing presses. So the Paarl, some thirty-six miles from Cape Town, had no press until 1876. A Paarl imprint of 1870 occurs on a Dutch catalogue of the library of the Rev. G. W. A. van der Lingen, noted on p. 270 of Th. Hahn's *Index of the Grey Collection in the South African Public Library*, but it was printed in Cape Town.

In 1876 P. J. Malherbe established a press in his father's house in the Paarl, and *De Christelyke School in hare Verhouding tot Kerk en Staat* (The Christian school in its relation to Church and State) as well as *De Kleine Schoorsteenveger* (The little chimney sweep) appeared in that year. At the beginning of 1877 the first Afrikaans newspaper, *Di Afrikaanse Patriot*, which had been printed by Smuts and Hofmeyr in Cape Town since its inception on 15 January 1876, was taken over by the printer in Paarl. It was printed on a small hand press, an Albion dating from 1869, and which has survived until today, and having been used in the film *Die Wonder van Afrikaans*

(The miracle of Afrikaans) is now in the Huguenot Museum in French Hoek, near Paarl.[1] The firm later was absorbed in D. F. du Toit & Co. This name appears in the imprint of most books of the earliest period of Afrikaans as a written language, and as the editions were small and the paper poor, comparatively few have survived the rigours of time. It was therefore most unexpected to find an Afrikaans publication of this press listed in 1927 in Southwark as the example for a book published in 1881 in an exhibition entitled *Four and a half Centuries of Printing*.[2] The first Afrikaans journal with any literary pretentions, *Ons Klynti* (The little one), was printed by this press in March 1896.

The name of H. Stroombergen[3] occurs on at least one book issued in the Paarl in 1877. He had apparently moved from Cape Town, as he is listed as a Cape Town compositor in issues of the the *Cape Almanac* between 1860 and 1865.

In 1877 G. M. Theal printed *Stories of the Amaxosa* at Alice, and in 1878 printing came to Oudtshoorn, when its first newspaper, *Oudtshoorn Courant*, appeared on 1 June.

Stellenbosch, although a university town since 1886, does not seem to have had a press of its own until the beginning of the twentieth century. The reason, no doubt, is its proximity to Cape Town, for it is only thirty miles away. Even Worcester, which is a hundred miles from Cape Town, did not have a newspaper until 13 May 1865, when *The Worcester Courant* was established.

In the Cape the earliest presses in use were small wooden ones; then came the Stanhope, and the Ruthven, and a little later, the Albion. In 1881 came the Wharfedale for the *Cape Times* during the second half of the last decade of the nineteenth century. These were the first rotary presses in the country. The first Linotype was, it is believed, imported into South Africa for the Grahamstown Exhibition, which opened on 1 January 1899. J. Appleton and T. Parrott were sent with this machine, and erected and supervised it. It was acquired by *Grocott's Penny Mail* in Grahamstown.[4] In the early years of the century individual printers placed their own orders with overseas firms for a supply of printing materials, but by 1880 William Foster

1. *Die Burger*, Cape Town, 17 May 1965.
2. Southwark Public Libraries & Cuming Museum. *Catalogue of an Exhibition of Four and a Half Centuries of Printing* ... October 7th, 1927, Item 1881 on p. 31.
3. Nienaber, P. J. *'n Beknopte Geskiedenis van die Hollands-Afrikaanse Drukpers in Suid-Afrika*. Kaapstad, Nasionale Pers, 1943, p. 112.
4. Downes, A. J. *Printers' Saga: being a History of the South African Typographical Union, etc.* Johannesburg, S.A.T.U., 1952, p. 89.

& Co., St. George's Street, Cape Town, advertised that they were agents for V. & J. Figgins, type founders, London, and that it was possible to supply printing presses, machines of every description, and all the necessary materials from stock.[1] By this time the type of advertisement taken from *The South African Chronicle*, 24 October 1826, seems to have disappeared from Cape papers:

Old Metal Types.
Well worth the attention of Printers, as a Remittance; or of Boers, for making Bullets for Elephant and other large Animal Shooting.

About 4000 lb. of the above for Sale by Auction at R. REEVES' Commission Sale, of *Wednesday* the first November. To be put up in convenient Lots.

1. *Afrikaanse Almanak*, 1880. Inside back cover.

Printing in Natal

Although Vasco da Gama had named the fertile country he gazed at from the sea on 25 December 1498 'in memory of the day when Christian men first saw it',[1] Natal was not inhabited by white men until the end of the first quarter of the nineteenth century. Printing was introduced by the American missionaries, and W. R. Morrison[2] says in 1838 by means of a hand press moved from place to place on a wagon.

The earliest reference to printing, as far as a commercial press in Natal is concerned, is the record of a request from C. P. Moll and C. E. Boniface to the Voortrekker Volksraad at Pietermaritzburg on 22 March 1844. They sought permission to print and publish a newspaper called *Natalier en Pietermarits Burg* [sic] *Getrouwe Aantekenaar* (The Natalian and Pietermaritzburg faithful recorder). Permission was granted on condition they provided certain securities. Boniface as editor obtained permission on 3 September 1844 to publish extracts from the Volksraad minutes, on condition that copies were made from the documents in the office, and nothing removed. To this condition Boniface remarked that as the offices were generally open at most for half an hour after the proceedings had been completed, the resolution as it stood was not of practical use to him.[3]

Both men came from Cape Town where they had been associated in publishing ventures, Moll evidently printing from 1833. Their Cape Town journal, *The Moderator* (later *De Meditator*) was not successful, and by April 1840 Moll was insolvent. He tried to make a living as a butcher, wagon-maker and smith, and even as an occasional journeyman for W. Buchanan of the *Cape Town Mail*.[4]

1. Theal, G. M. *History of South Africa before 1795* ... 3rd ed. London, George Allen & Unwin, vol. 1, p. 58.
2. Morrison, W. R. 'A Bibliographical Excursion' in *South African Libraries*, vol. 4, p. 36.
3. Union of South Africa. *S.A. Archival Records: Natal*, vol. 1, p. 226 n.
4. Nienaber, G. S. *Van Roem tot Selfmoord.* Johannesburg, Voortrekkerspers, 1939, p. 81.

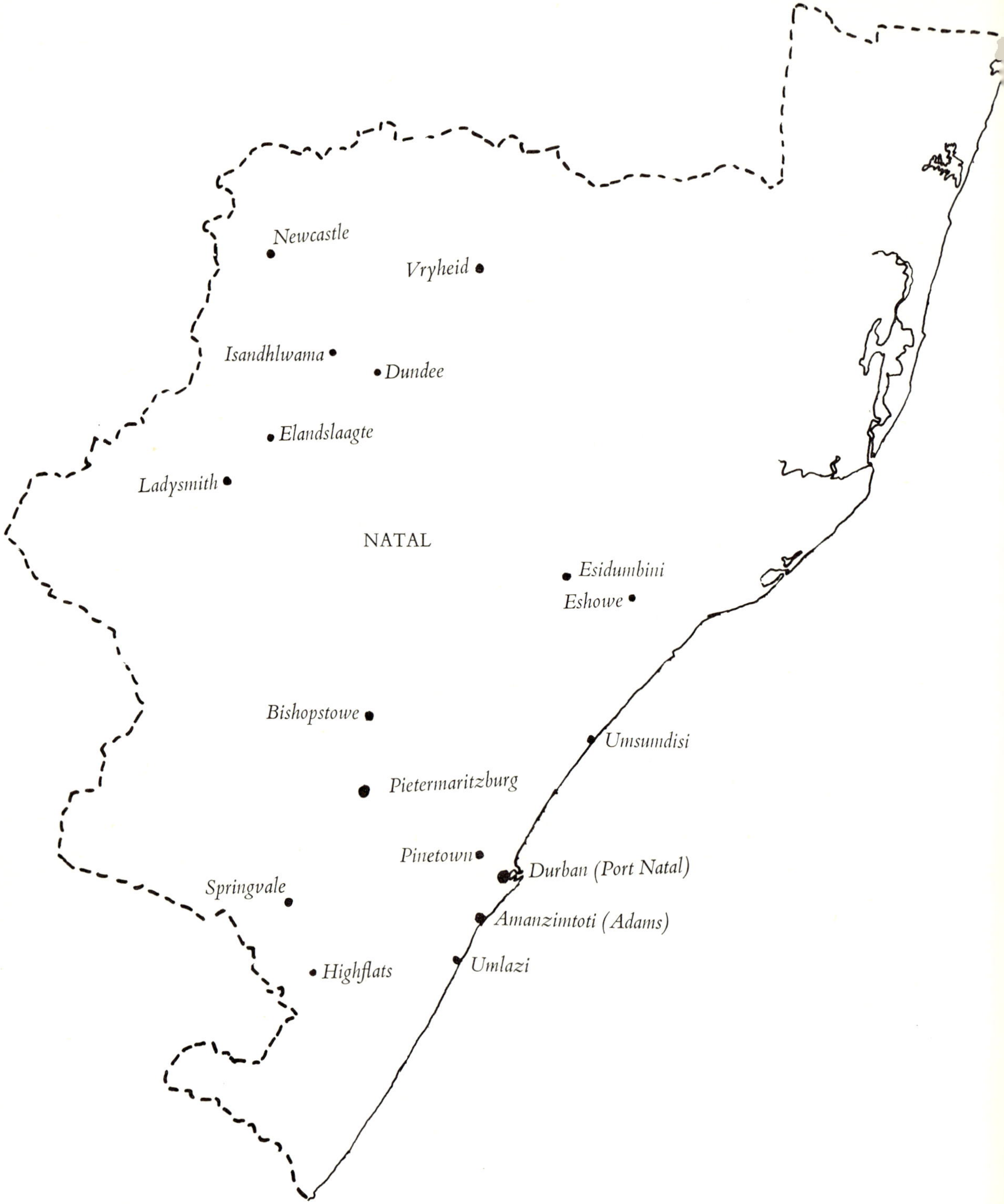
Newcastle
Vryheid
Isandhlwama
Dundee
Elandslaagte
Ladysmith
NATAL
Esidumbini
Eshowe
Bishopstowe
Umsumdisi
Pietermaritzburg
Pinetown
Durban (Port Natal)
Springvale
Amanzimtoti (Adams)
Umlazi
Highflats

Moll and Boniface left for Natal on 16 February 1844 intending to set up a printing works in Durban, and presumably taking a press with them for this purpose. On arrival, they decided to go to Pietermaritzburg instead of Durban. They went to live in a house in Pietermaritzburg at 22 Church Street, where half the house was occupied by the printing works. Their newspaper appeared on 19 April 1844, and they were fined £100 by the Landdrost because their paper appeared on Saturday and not Friday as stipulated in their agreement. Moll and Boniface fell out, and Arthur Walker became editor on 21 April 1846. Because of legal proceedings, Natal's first paper the weekly, *De Natalier*, ceased on 29 September 1846.

Hattersley quoting *The Natal Witness* of 7 March 1876, reports that *De Natalier* appeared regularly unless the publisher found it convenient to postpone publication or even to skip a week. The editor was C. E. Boniface, who was also reporter and book-keeper, while the foreman, news and job printer, and printer's devil was Cornelius Moll, 'a clever gentleman who wrote excellent articles in Dutch and English. Joshua Kincaid was the motive power than ran the press'.[1] The circulation was extensive—all of forty. Some weeks the paper would appear on ordinary printing paper, then for a couple of issues on elegant cream-laid, 'then it would bloom for a while on red-tinted paper, with a change to yellow and a final resolve into green; and when the stock of coloured and white paper ran out, a foraging party after wrapping paper and stray grocery bags' was sent out. From this it is clear that the *Natalier* had a somewhat chequered career. Some copies have survived in the Durban Municipal Library and the Natal Archives in Pietermaritzburg, and so have copies of the next bilingual weekly paper which started in Pietermaritzburg on 4 December 1846 and in which Walker and Moll were again associated. It was first called *The* (or *De*) *Patriot*, and then, on 19 November 1847, the *Natal Patriot*. It moved to Durban in 1848, where it ceased in July 1848. The Rev. James Archbell (1798–1866) who had been Wesleyan missionary, and had printed at Maquassi and Platberg went to Natal in 1842, and was associated with various Natal newspapers, such as *The Natal Independent*, *The Times*, *The Natal Guardian* and the *Natal Courier*. There must have been some contact between Moll and Archbell, for the paper the *Natal en Zuid-Oost Afrikaan* established on 2 April 1853 in Durban by Archbell was transferred to Pietermaritzburg on 7 October 1853, where it became the *Zuid-Oost Afrikaan* (the South-east African) and where Moll appar-

1. Hattersley, A. F. *The Natalians: further Annals of Natal, etc.* Pietermaritzburg, Shuter & Shooter 1940, p. 146–148.

ently printed it until it ceased supposedly on 17 August 1855, the date of the latest surviving issue in the Natal Archives. It is also on record that after Moll was released from prison, Thomas Phipson, who managed Archbell's *Natal Independent*, employed Moll in Durban, and dismissed him 'for incompetency to conduct the printing office and bad temper'.[1]

It would seem that official publications were among the earliest to be issued in Pietermaritzburg, as *Rules, Orders and Regulations, respecting the Manner and Form of Proceeding in Civil and Criminal Cases*, etc. is dated 1847, and *The Municipal Regulations for the Town of Pietermaritzburg*, bears the date 1848 and D. D. Buchanan as printer.

If Moll was in and out of gaol, so was, though for other reasons, David Dale Buchanan, who landed in Cape Town in December 1829, worked for the *Cape Town Mail*, and arrived in Natal in January 1846 with 'a fount of old battered type and a half worn-out hand press', given to him by the *Cape Town Mail*. Buchanan and an African assistant launched *The Natal Witness* in Pietermaritzburg on 27 February 1846 as a free weekly bilingual news sheet of four pages. They worked in one room in a house opposite the Market Square in Church Street. Today this is South Africa's oldest paper, as it has appeared continuously since it was established.

Buchanan inaugurated his own postal service between Pietermaritzburg and Durban in order that his paper should get news and wide distribution, for at that time there was no postal service between these places. As his native runners were faster than an ox wagon, Buchanan carried letters for others at sixpence a time. At first one runner did the trip there and back once a week, but later two runners were employed, one starting from each end, exchanging bags at Inchanga, and then returning to the place from which they had come. Still later wagonettes were used.[2] When Durban and Pietermaritzburg were connected by telegraph in 1865, and a cable was laid between Durban and (Portuguese) Lourenço Marques in 1879, the need for Buchanan's service fell away.

It is on record that on 26 October 1848 Buchanan complained that he could not get apprentices. Parents in the Natal of those days felt that other trades offered better prospects than that of printing.

By 1849 new offices were required for *The Natal Witness* and the staff was soon to consist of a Mr. Wagner (presumably A. J. Wagner, who later worked at Potchef-

1. Nienaber, G. S. *Van Roem tot Selfmoord*. Johannesburg, Voortrekker pers, 1939, p. 133.
2. Rose, F. H. 'Progress of the "Press"' in *A Century of Progress in Natal, 1824–1924:* being the centenary number of *The Natal Witness*, p. 81–88.

stroom in the Transvaal); two apprentices called Osborne and Holgate,[1] and two printers, John May and Peter Davis. The last two took over from Buchanan, when his legal practice and public duties began to demand more of his time. He became Pietermaritzburg's first Mayor in 1854, a Member of the Legislative Council of Natal, and died in Cape Town on 4 September 1874.

Early in March 1876 a flag and pennant were hoisted over the *Witness* office in Longmarket Street, Pietermaritzburg, to herald the introduction of the first machinery driven printing press.[2]

By 1879 *The Natal Witness* was published twice a week in an edition of 500 copies and printed on a Belle Sauvage press.[3] By 1881 it was a daily, and John May had long ceased to be an owner, but Peter Davis went on until 1916. He had had a London training as a compositor, was a keen businessman known for brusqueness of manner and a dislike of trade unions, but he undoubtedly wielded great influence, and played an important part in the newspaper world of South Africa. He died on 7 May 1919 aged eighty-two.

On 29 August 1851 two papers made their appearance in Durban—Edward Scott's *D'Urban* [sic] *Observer and Natal General Advertiser* and Jeremiah Cullingworth's *Natal Times*. Hattersley[4] says Cullingworth was first, and McKinnell[5] says Scott was first. Downes[6] unfortunately has the names of the papers wrong, but there probably is some truth in the story which survived among printers that Scott beat Cullingworth by two hours and that his victory was celebrated by a banquet at an hotel.

Edward Scott was the printer, and the owners were Leonard Wray and a certain Mr. James. Scott later became editor as well. It was a four-page weekly and ceased in 1852, when Scott started the *D'Urban* [sic] *Advocate and General Advertiser*, which lasted until 1854. Whether the E. Scott listed as a compositor in the *Natal Almanac* for 1887 is the same man is doubtful, as Edward Scott is reported to have sold his plant in 1854.

1. Hattersley, A. F. *The Natalians: further Annals of Natal, etc.* Pietermaritzburg, Shuter & Shooter, 1940, p. 147–148.
2. McKinnell, R. T. 'The Printing and Newspaper Industry of South Africa with special reference to Natal' [Unpublished M. A. thesis, University of Natal, December 1951], p. 12.
3. *South African Typographical Journal*, March 1930, p. 6.
4. Hattersley, A. F. 'Byways of South African Journalism in Early Victorian Days', in *Quarterly Bulletin of the S.A. Library*, December 1956, p. 54.
5. McKinnell, R. T. 'The Printing and Newspaper Industry of South Africa with special reference to Natal'. [Unpublished M.A. thesis, University of Natal, December 1951], p. 9.
6. Downes, A. J. *Printers' Saga, etc.* Johannesburg, S.A.T.U., 1952, p. 11.

The *Natal Times* was a quaint production of four small pages of which copies have survived. The editor was Frederick Kinloch, and it was published twice a week. It stopped shortly after the *Natal Mercury* started on 25 November 1852. Cullingworth also printed the early issues of the *Natal Mercury*, although the owner was George Robinson, father of the late Sir John, who himself wrote the editorials, until he became Prime Minister of Natal. The press used by Cullingworth was a small Eagle which is preserved by the *Natal Mercury*. The Robinsons also took over the printing material of the defunct *Advertiser* in August 1855 and of the *Commercial Advertiser* in September 1860. Until 1898 the *Mercury* was still being set by hand—said to be the only paper so set in Natal at the time. In 1899 a rotary press was installed.

Jeremiah Cullingworth was born in Leeds in 1807 where he was a printer and stationer before coming to Natal in 1850 with his wife and seven children. He also brought with him a Britannia press of the model invented by B. Porter. It has been preserved in the Durban Museum. This press was not only used to print the *Natal Times*, but also for such jobbing printing as came the firm's way. It was only at the turn of the century that newspapers began to give up jobbing printing, when general commercial printers became available to do this type of work.

Cullingworth was responsible for the *Port Natal Almanac*, and printed a Zulu Vocabulary and Phrase Book that went into many editions after its first appearance in 1850. On 22 August 1855 he established *The Natal Star*, which lasted at least until 1862, in which year he is recorded as printing a map. At the end of the century, the printing business was in the hands of a son, T. L. Cullingworth, as the founder had died in 1887.

At the beginning of the twentieth century Durban could boast seven printing firms among which were T. L. Cullingworth, P. Davis & Sons, and Robinson & Co.

It may be of interest to note the opinion of the newspapers of Pietermaritzburg as recorded by a visitor who left England on 22 June 1850:[1]

> There were two newspapers in Maritzburg. If any of my readers wish to know what sort of a thing a colonial newspaper is, I cannot do better than refer them to the pages of 'Pickwick', where they will find an apt representation, not the least exaggerated, in the *Eatanswill Gazette* and *Inde-*

1. Barter, C. *The Dorp and the Veld; or, Six Months in Natal, etc.* London, William S. Orr, 1852, p. 186–187. The 'Project' mentioned by Barter refers to the proposal to send a force of Zulus to assist Sir Harry Smith on the Cape Frontier.

pendent. Mr. Pott and his antagonist, of *buff* notoriety, will stand very well for the respective editors, who were of course at daggers drawn, and who, if they did not actually belabour one another with carpet bags and broomsticks, yet contrived to carry on a very pretty duello with the goose-quill which they wielded with tremendous effect. The interesting details of the warfare, varied by unsparing attacks upon all constitutional authorities, and enlivened by a happy mixture of personal abuse and private scandal, made their clamours on the whole excessively piquant and entertaining. Even with all these attractions however, to say nothing of the satirical pieces by the colonial Byron, the sonnets by the young Minerva, whom nobody could identify, and the spirited advertisements, master-pieces in the puff style, by our George Robins, whom not to know was to be unknown, the want of novelty would sometimes make itself felt, and it may easily be imagined with what avidity a topic of such universal interest, and affording such ample field for discussion as the Lieutenant-Governor's project, was seized upon by the rival dignitaries of the Maritzburg press. The *Natal Witness* was first in the field, and took up the opposition side with such rabid violence as almost to defeat its own object, by shaming all but the most shameless into something like a spirit of loyalty, and alienating from its party all the respectable portion of the populace, whose organ it affected to be. Had her Majesty's representative been set in the pillory, as the butt for plebeian insolence and rotten eggs, he could not have been assailed by coarser witticisms, or pelted with a greater collection of filth, than was hurled at his devoted head from the printing-office in 'Church Street'. I need scarcely say, that Mr. Pine treated all these attacks with the contempt they deserved, and that their effect was rather to increase than to diminish his popularity; but one could not help doubting whether, after all, the boasted liberty of the press might not be a questionable advantage, and sighing for the revival of some good old law for slitting the ears of impertinent slanderers.

It is to be hoped that Charles Barter avoided all these pitfalls when he edited *The Natal Guardian*, an Anglican church weekly in support of Bishop Colenso. The first issue appeared on 8 January 1856, and the last one recorded in the Natal Archives is dated April 1857. The publisher was James Archbell of Pietermaritzburg.

There were a few other church magazines both in Dutch and in English, such as *De Natal Bode* (The Natal Messenger) from 17 February 1862 to 29 December 1862 and *The Natal Magazine* (1878–1879), but none appear to have survived for any length of time. The same is true of the literary and general journals such as *The Natal Journal* (1857–1858), a quarterly miscellany of literature and science.

Except for Pietermaritzburg and Durban, very little printing seems to have been done by ordinary presses in the towns of Natal during the nineteenth century. Cornelius Moll and his old hand press were associated with *De Ware Patriot* in Ladysmith. It is believed that it started on 20 or 26 November 1856 and lasted about six months, probably until Moll left for the Transvaal. The only copies known are in the Natal Archives. It was published once a week and was in Dutch only.

The Argus Annual of 1889 lists *Natal Record* as a fortnightly owned by F. Pfarmer of Pine Town, but nothing more is known of this publication, and it is therefore not possible to say whether it is the first printing in Pine Town.

In the 'eighties Newcastle had two newspapers. As the starting dates are not known for either, it is not possible to say exactly when printing started in this town, but as the surviving copies of the *Newcastle Echo* are dated October 1881 to 1884, and the *Newcastle Herald* is not mentioned until 29 December 1885, when an advertisement for a Clerk to the Village Board[1] was to be inserted in the paper, the assumption is that, if these journals were printed in Newcastle from the start, the earliest printing in this town is not later than October 1881, but it may have been as early as 1875. Haddon & Co. are mentioned as the owners of the *Newcastle Echo* in its earliest years.[2] In 1882 a pamphlet, *Natal and Responsible Government*, was reprinted from the paper by C. W. Deecker at the Newcastle Echo office. Deecker later went to the Transvaal.

Finally there is Vryheid, which at one stage in its history belonged to the Transvaal, but is here conveniently considered with Natal. Between 28 January 1892 and 26 September 1899 a newspaper appeared every week in this town. It was called *De Nieuwe Republikein* until 11 January 1899, when it became *De Republikein*. It seems to have been in Dutch only. It obviously ceased publication because the South African War had broken out. The *Anglo-African Who's Who* for 1910 records that Alexander von Levetzow, born in Neuhoff, Mecklenburg-Schwerin, was a member of the old Transvaal Civil Service from 1878 to 1885 and Magistrate at Vryheid from 1885 to 1887, where he edited and published the *Nieuwe Republikein*. Whether he actually printed is not known. He was still active in 1893, for he is recorded as the publisher in Vryheid of J. H. Hattingh's *De Geschiedenis van de Hollandsch-Afrikaansche Boeren, vanaf hun Vertrek uit de Kaapkolonie, tot op de Aftreding van President Burgers* (The history of the Dutch-Afrikaans Boers from their departure from the Cape Colony to the retirement of President Burgers).[3] This is one of the comparatively small number of books or pamphlets with the names of places in Natal other than Durban or Pietermaritzburg in their imprints.

Although there were many Indians in Natal, an Indian printing press was not established until 1899, and so hardly comes into this survey.

1. Baylis, B. C. *A History of Newcastle*. Newcastle, Newcastle Advertiser, 1951, vol. 1, p. 39.
2. *Ibidem*, Vol. 1, p. 31.
3. Nienaber, P. J. *'n Beknopte Geskiedenis van die Hollands-Afrikaanse Drukpers in Suid-Afrika*. Kaapstad, Nasionale Pers, 1943, p. 82.

Robert Patrick, one of the early active trade unionists in Natal, recounted the founding of the first union in Natal as follows:

In 1884 piece-work had been established in Natal. The scale of prices for the various fonts were not satisfactory. In Capetown ls. per 1,000 ens was being paid. In Natal a sliding scale was introduced and 11d. per 1,000 was the highest for minion. Brevier followed at 10 d., bourgeois at 9d., long primer at 8½d. and small pica at 8d.

In 1888 Messrs. Banwell, Glanville, Empey, McKillop, Clowes, Elliott, Tarr, Bowden and Robert Patrick met at the house of the convenor (Robert Patrick) to discuss the formation of a Society.

Rules were drafted out. The election of the Executive was: Henry Banwell (Chairman), J. R. Glanville (Vice-Chairman), Robert Patrick, Secretary and Treasurer. Committee: Empey, Clowes, Elliott, Bowden, McKillop and Tarr. The subscription was fixed at 6d. per week and a collector appointed in each office. Membership included every branch of the Printing Trade—the total membership in Durban was 41.

The Secretary was sent to Maritzburg to form a branch there and a meeting was called on a Saturday evening at the Crown Hotel, at which practically everyone employed in the industry was present and it was unanimously carried to join the young Society. Mr. C. V. Borain was appointed Secretary and a committee appointed.

The Natal Typographical Society now set to work—a rise in wages was secured—assisted passages to skilled artisans by the European Emigration Board was abolished–the stoppage of Government printing from overseas was accomplished. The Natal Railways established their own Printing Works. The Corporations of Durban and Maritzburg also stopped printing from overseas. The Natal membership increased rapidly.[1]

1. *South African Typographical Journal*, June 1933, p. 23.

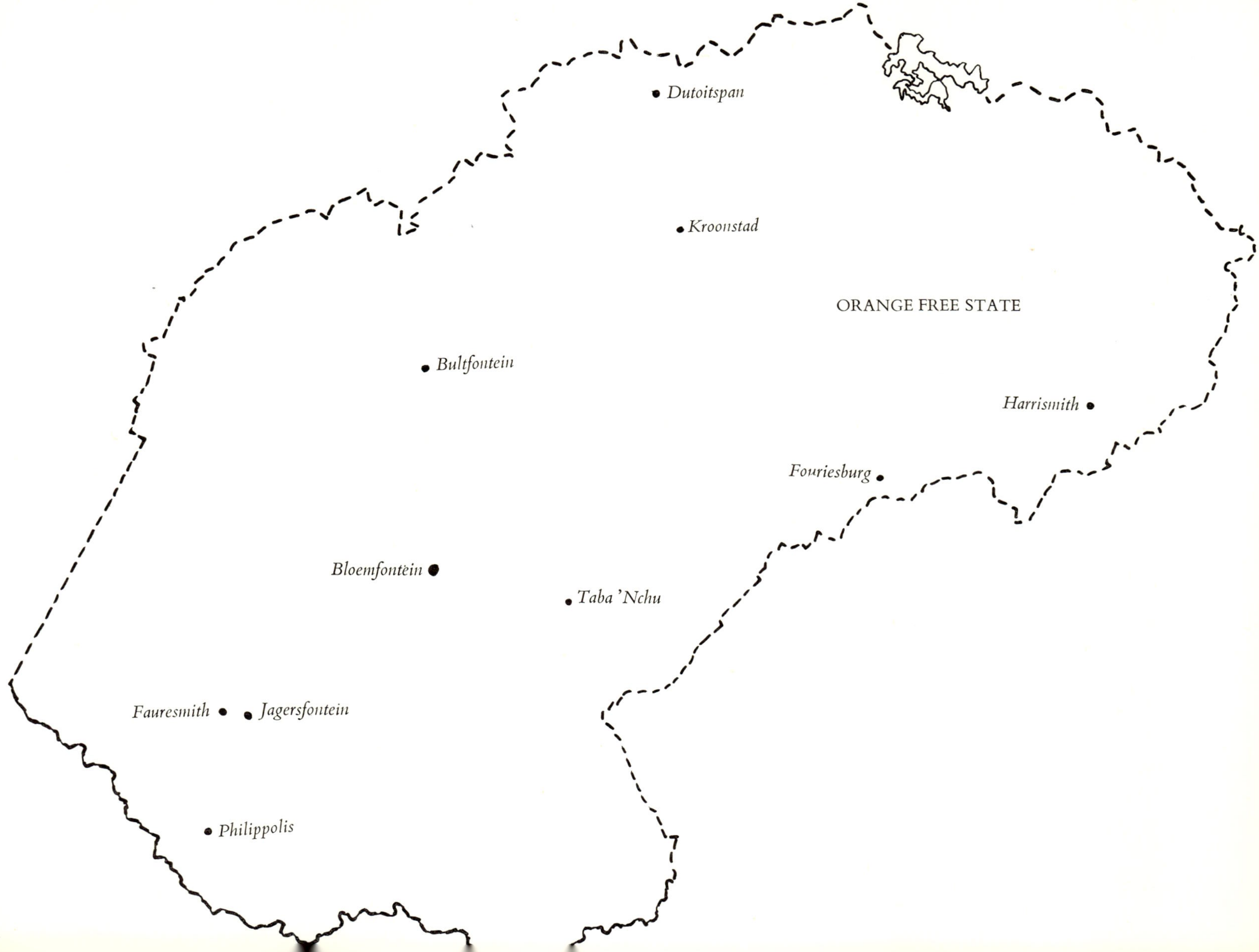
Dutoitspan
Kroonstad
ORANGE FREE STATE
Bultfontein
Harrismith
Fouriesburg
Bloemfontein
Taba 'Nchu
Fauresmith
Jagersfontein
Philippolis

Printing in the Orange Free State

Although hunters and explorers had crossed the Orange River into the area today known as the Orange Free State, the settled population was sparse and rural even by the middle of the nineteenth century. The capital city, Bloemfontein, only dated from 1846, and here on 10 June 1850, *The Friend of the Sovereignty and Bloem Fontein Gazette/Vriend van de Souwereiniteit en Bloem Fonteinse Courant* was established as a bilingual weekly. It is the only example in South Africa where the first paper to appear in any one of the Provinces has survived until the present day. To celebrate its centenary, a special supplement was issued, and the following chronology is part of that which was published on the occasion:

1850, March 16: Messrs. Godlonton and White write to the Governor of the Cape, Sir Harry Smith, asking for permission to 'establish a Printing Office at Bloem Fontein'.

1850, June 10: First issue of *The Friend of the Sovereignty and Bloem Fontein Gazette.*

1850, September: Nathaniel William Barlow joins Editorial staff.

1854, February 23: Bloemfontein Convention—the Sovereignty abandoned.

1854: Thomas White becomes proprietor as well as Editor, and is assisted by Nathaniel William Barlow.

1854, August 5: Paper's name changed to *The Friend of the Free State.*

1854, September 18: Dutch takes precedence over English in the presentation of the paper.

1855, February 17: President Hoffman resigns. First record of Parliamentary reporting in *The Friend.*

1855: Alfred Barlow joins staff of the paper.

1862, October 20: *De Tijd*, first opposition to *The Friend* appears.

1865, August 20: Basuto War. Report of the Battle of Thaba Bosigo. Wilhelm Hoevels, correspondent of *The Friend* killed and J. M. Howell, another correspondent, injured.

1872: Thomas White takes the Barlow brothers into partnership.

1875, January: *De Tijd* ceases publication.

1875, March 11: *The Express and Orange Free State Advertiser* appears in opposition to *The Friend.*

1876, July: Thomas White dies in London. Alfred Barlow was head of *The Friend* and practically

Editor as well. Nathaniel William Barlow meanwhile acts as 'Sporting Editor' and as 'Political Editor.' Both Alfred and Nathaniel William act as Editors, but Alfred very much in control. The firm now becomes Barlow Bros. & Co., the brothers having equal shares, including Herbert Barlow, the non-journalist in the family.

1876, July 27: First telegrams appear in *The Friend.*

1882, July: *The Express* becomes *The Daily News.*

1888: Death of Nathaniel William Barlow in Cape Town. Alfred and Herbert continue in partnership, Alfred retaining Editorial control.

1890, August 15: *The Friend of the Free State* becomes bi-weekly.

1890: *The Daily News* reverts to its old name of *The Express.*

1891: Herbert Barlow leaves for England permanently.

1894, January 1: *De Burger,* all-Dutch publication by Barlow Brothers appears.

1894, January 2: *The Friend of the Free State* appears all in English and reduced in size.

1896. March 16: *The Daily Friend* appears and *The Friend of the Free State* continues as bi-weekly.

1897: Arthur G. Barlow takes over from his father, who joins the Board. December 29: *De Burger* ceases publication.

1899, September 29: *The Friend* supports Volksraad in its decision to go to war, though this is opposed to the paper's policy.

The name of the paper was originally chosen as a compliment to the Cape Governor, Sir Harry Smith, who permitted the owners to establish the paper. The reference was to *The Friend of India* and to the Governor's military exploits in India. During the first few years before the establishment of the *Gouvernements Courant* (Government gazette) on 10 March 1857, *The Friend* served as an official gazette in which proclamations and government notices were published.[1] The Centenary Supplement to *The Friend* quotes as follows from the memorandum Sir Harry Smith had received from the Colonial Office, when he obtained permission for Godlonton and White to establish the newspaper: official matter 'not to exceed the first two pages—each page to contain three columns in English and to be printed on the same sized paper as the Cape Town Gazette—and an equal quantity of matter in the Dutch language'. The type for all official matter was to be Small Pica, and the printers were to supply 250 copies of the *Gazette* free of charge, for which an annual grant of £100 was to be made. Extra copies were to be supplied at threepence each, and any official matter exceeding the quantity stipulated was to be charged at the rate of fifteen shillings a column. The firm was also to be Government Stationer and Printer for the Orange Free State.

In Grahamstown an old hand press, cases of type (including the Pica decreed by

1. Union of South Africa. Archives Commission. *South African Archival Records: Orange Free State,* vol. 1, p. xl.

Whitehall), paper, etc. etc. were loaded on an ox wagon to set up the first commercial printing works north of the Orange River. The press was the one Godlonton had taken over from Meurant, in other words, the old Settlers' press from Graaff Reinet. It is believed that a part of it is still in possession of *The Friend*.

Thomas Baines, the traveller and artist, spent some weeks in 1850 in the printing office of *The Friend* making woodcuts out of firewood which were used to illustrate the paper shortly after it was established.[1] *The Friend* was therefore early with pictures made in South Africa.

The papers noted in the chronology compiled by *The Friend* were all issued in Bloemfontein. There were, however, a few sporadic attempts to establish newspapers and printing presses in some other towns of the Orange Free State before the end of the nineteenth century, but very few, if any, copies of these publications have survived until today.

Excluding the mission stations, such as Philippolis with its *Dagster* (Morning Star) in 1859, Fauresmith seems to have been first in the field with *Vrystaat Burgher*, which is mentioned in the *Cape Almanac* for 1872 as being published every Tuesday. Otherwise nothing is known about it. The assumption is that it was printed at Fauresmith and that this town therefore was the first to have a printing press outside Bloemfontein, but there is, of course, the possibility that Fauresmith, like Harrismith with its *Harrismith Times* of 1862, was satisfied with a handwritten paper. Harrismith was indeed next with a printing press, for in January 1882 A. W. Bayly and a certain Mackay established a bilingual weekly. *The Harrismith Chronicle. The Friend* of 12 January 1882 reported that a copy of the first issue printed on white satin was given to President Brand. Presentation addresses and programmes were then frequently printed on satin in South Africa. *The Harrismith Chronicle* is listed in the *Cape Almanac* for 1883, and only lasted until September of that year.[2] Arthur William Bayly was born in Southampton in 1855, and came to South Africa in 1879. *The Harrismith Chronicle* was his first South African paper, but he was later engaged in printing papers in Barberton and Lourenço Marques. The plant of *The Harrismith Chronicle*, remained in the town and was used by Francis Mandy for *The Free State Chronicle*, which ran from November 1883 until November 1884.

John Scoble edited two papers published in Jagersfontein in the early 'eighties, but nothing much is known about them except their names—*The Breakfast Table*, a

1. Gray, J. *Payable Gold, etc.* South Africa, Central News Agency, 1937, p. 16.
2. Steytler, F. A. *Die Geskiedenis van Harrismith* (Bloemfontein, Nasionale Pers, pref. 1932), p. 114

daily lasting only a few weeks, and *The Free State Argus*, with only a brief life.[1] Two, unfortunately unidentified, but contemporary, newscuttings are both uncomplimentary to these two papers. The first quotes 'Eighty-one-Tonner' as writing: 'I saw a few copies of the *Breakfast Table*. It would be a splendid medium for conveying the shaving paste from one's razor to the slop bucket, provided it were supplied gratis!' The other cutting concerns *The Free State Argus* as an 'apparently irresponsible Jagersfontein contemporary'. These cuttings were collected by Norwood Coaker, some time editor of *The Mining Record and Jagersfontein Advertiser*, and are now housed in the Johannesburg Public Library.

Free State material has rarely survived the years, and it is therefore not unexpected to find that almanacs, annuals, and journals, published before 1900, are in most cases known only through notices in *The Friend* or other newspapers.

Paul Combes in compiling information for *Cent Ans de Lutte les Héros Boers*, received the following reply from President F. W. Reitz[2] in response to a request for details on the progress of printing in the Orange Free State:

> Répondant à votre lettre du mois de novembre 1894 me demandant des renseignements sur la presse dans cet État, je regrette de vous informer qu'ici la presse est à peine sortie de l'enfance.
>
> Les seuls journaux qui se publient sont le *Friend of the Free State*, qui commença à paraître en 1860, et l'*Express*, qui ne date que de 1874. Ces deux journaux sont publieés, partie en anglais, partie en néerlandais.
>
> Le pays est, en effet, virtuellement bilingue, la population rurale employant principalement le néerlandais que est la langue du gouvernement, tandis que les habitants des villes employent l'anglais.
>
> La *Government Gazette* (journal officiel), est publiée en néerlandais et date de la constitution de la République comme État indépendant, c'est-à-dire de 1854.
>
> Il n'y a presque aucun livre publié ici, sauf une *Géographie et Histoire de l'État libre d'Orange* publiée pour les écoles par MM. C. Borkenhagen et Co en 1892. La même maison a publié, la même année, les *Lois de l'État* en un fort beau volume in-8° d'environ 800 pages.
>
> Les *Minutes du Volksraad* ont été publiées annuellement depuis 1854, et constituent trente-huit volumes in-8° de 300 à 400 pages chacun.
>
> De nombreuses brochures contenant les rapports des commissions nommées par le Volksraad ont été aussi publiées par les deux imprimeries de Bloemfontein, celle du *Friend* et celle de l'*Express.*
>
> On a essayé, de temps en temps, de faire paraître des journaux dans diverses localités de la République, comme le *Northern Post*, à Harrismith, le *Jagersfontein Herald*, aux mines de diamant de Jagersfontein, mais ils sont morts de mort naturelle après peu de temps.

1. *Men of the Times: Pioneers of the Transvaal and Glimpses of South Africa.* [Johannesburg?], Transvaal Publishing Co., 1905, p. 329.
2. Combes, P. *Cent Ans de Lutte les Héros Boers, etc.* Paris, Montgredien, [1900?], p. 303.

Printing in the Transvaal

The first review of the progress of printing in the Orange Free State was undertaken to answer an overseas enquiry dated November 1894. In the Transvaal also, the first history of printing was occasioned by a question from an overseas correspondent. Dr. F. V. Engelenburg, Editor of the Pretoria newspaper *De Volkstem*, was asked to undertake the task, and his reply in Dutch, dated 6 May 1893, to the State Secretary, has survived in the Transvaal Archives, while a revised version in French is to be found in *Cent Ans de Lutte les Héros Boers*,[1] the publication for which both surveys were apparently undertaken.

Towards the middle of the nineteenth century there were various communities of Boers settled in different parts of the area to the north of the Vaal River in the country known today as the Transvaal. In the official papers and documents which have survived from this period the earliest reference to printing is to be found in a letter from Amsterdam dated 9 December 1850 from J. Schutte Hoyman asking for appointment as printer. On 4 December 1851 the Volksraad at Lydenburg agreed to appointing him State Printer for twenty-five years, but nothing more is heard of this proposal. On 20 March 1851 A. J. Wagner (possibly a printer from Natal) wrote to General A. W. J. Pretorius on the necessity of having a press, and suggested that money should be collected from the public for a community press. On 11 May 1851 Wagner wrote to the President once more to say that he was glad that Pretorius was successful in getting a press at Magaliesberg. Nothing came of any of these proposals.[2] Pretorius himself was most anxious to obtain a press, and approached P. A. Brand of Cape Town, who declined on financial grounds. On 20 November 1853 Landdrost (Magistrate) A. A. Smit of Potchefstroom requested a

1. Combes, P. *Cent Ans de Lutte les Héros Boers, etc.* p. 295–303.
2. Pelzer, A. N. *Geskiedenis van die Suid-Afrikaanse Republiek, etc.* Kaapstad, A. A. Balkema, 1950, deel 1, p. 161–162.

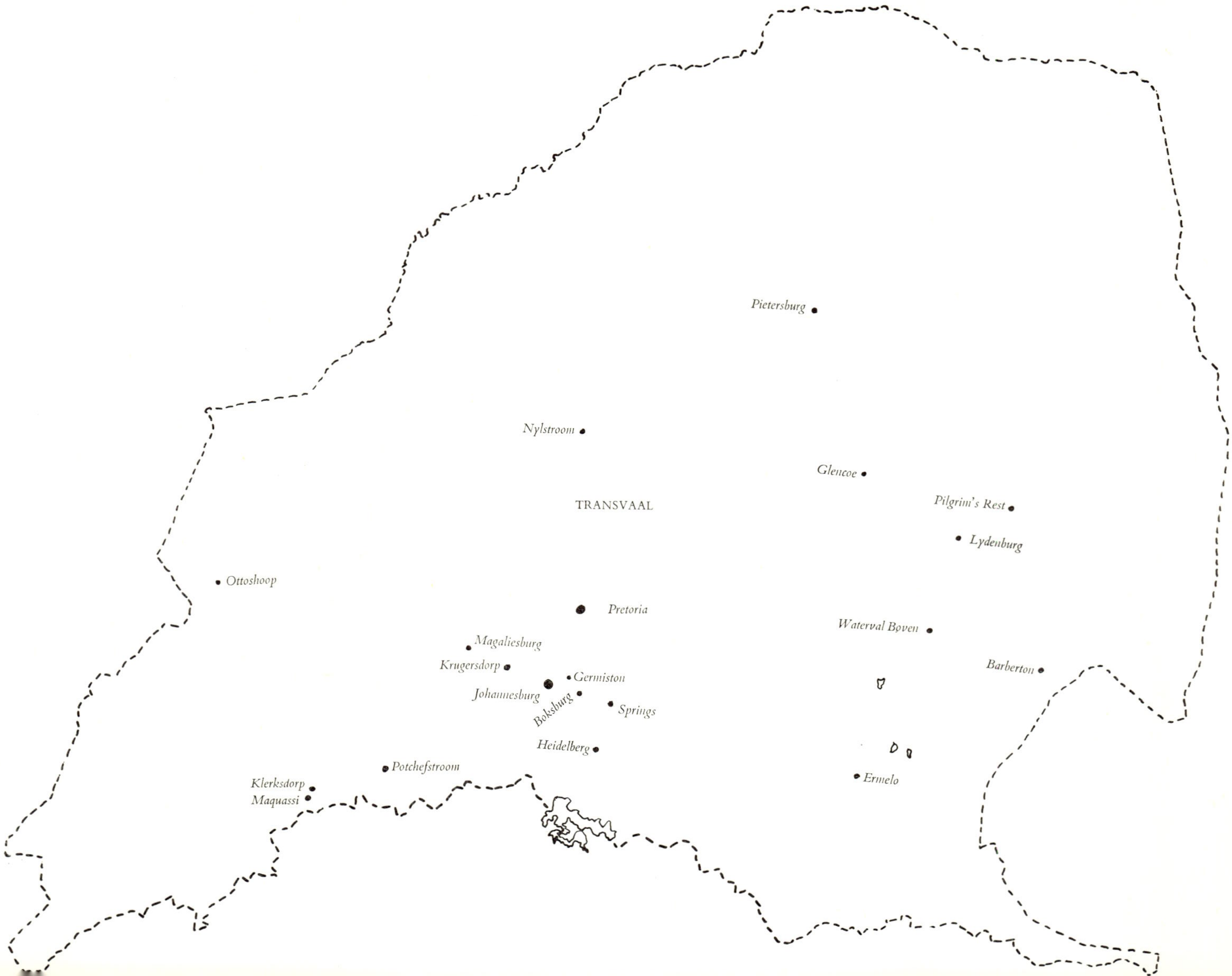
Pietersburg
Nylstroom
Glencoe
TRANSVAAL
Pilgrim's Rest
Lydenburg
Ottoshoop
Pretoria
Waterval Boven
Magaliesburg
Krugersdorp
Germiston
Barberton
Johannesburg
Boksburg
Springs
Heidelberg
Potchefstroom
Klerksdorp
Maquassi
Ermelo

press at Potchefstroom 'in order to promote the interests of the Republic and to civilise the people of the country'.[1] There was a rumour (though false) that Pretorius's opponent was getting a press from Holland. On 18 November 1852 C. P. Moll asked Andries Pretorius what the prospects were for a printer in the Transvaal, but it was only in July 1857 that Moll arrived in Potchefstroom with his plant. On 21 September 1857 Moll signed the contract to print a weekly *Government Gazette* of four pages making twelve columns for £100 a year, and to sell a maximum of eighty copies per week to the Government at threepence each. The *Gazette* was to be similar in shape and size to that being published in Natal. On 25 September 1857 the first issue appeared. As Moll was allowed to include unofficial matter, there soon was trouble and even a court case, as Moll did not always see eye to eye with the Government, and had no compunction in putting his views in the *Gazette*. A new arrangement was made. The Government purchased Moll's plant for £650 and retained his services as printer, but not as editor of the *Government Gazette*. H. Jeppe was appointed as editor. The Volksraad expressed the wish that everything possible should be done to establish a private newspaper.[2] On 17 December 1858 the *Staats Courant* (Government gazette) devoted a leader of more than a page to the importance of a newspaper for the dissemination of knowledge, and announced the publication of *De Republiek van Zuid-Afrika* (the republic of South Africa). It appeared on 4 February 1859, and by 15 October of that year had changed its name to *De Oude Emigrant* (the old emigrant).[3] Moll and Hermann Jeppe were associated with this paper, which appeared at Potchefstroom for about two years.

Cornelius Petrus Moll, who introduced printing into both Natal and the Transvaal, was born in Cape Town in 1810, where he presumably learnt the art of printing. His Cape Town imprint reads 'C. Moll, Junior', but by the time he was at work in the Transvaal he had become 'C. Moll, Senior'. The 'C. Moll, Junior' in Transvaal imprints refers to his eldest son of the same name, who also was a printer and whose name appears on early Transvaal *Government Gazettes*, for he was at work with his father at Potchefstroom. Moll Senior became State Secretary in the Transvaal—possibly that is the reason why his son's name occurs early as printer of the *Gazette*—and later Moll Senior was Landdrost (or Magistrate) first of Pretoria, and, at

1. Union of South Africa. Archives Commission. *South African Archival Records: Transvaal*, vol. 2, p. 530.
2. *Ibidem*, Vol. 4, p. 24.
3. Bosman, F. C. L. *Hollandse Joernalistiek in Suid-Afrika gedurende die 19de eeu, etc.* (Kaapstad, Federale Drukpers Maats.), [1930?], p. 12.

the time of his death in Nylstroom on 25 April 1880, of the Waterberg district.[1]

Late in 1861 Johannes Philippus Borrius, who was born in Amsterdam on 23 May 1840 and had worked in the Cape since 1860, first for Van de Sandt de Villiers, and then for Pike and Byles, arrived in Potchefstroom, where he was engaged by H. Jeppe to work on *De Oude Emigrant* and the *Government Gazette*. These were difficult days in the Transvaal with internal dissent and strife, and the press at Potchefstroom did not escape unscathed. It would seem as if *De Oude Emigrant* ceased in 1861 because of political pressure. It is on record that a certain Mr. James, the English editor of *De Oude Emigrant*, fled to Harrismith when trouble came. Whether the following anecdote[2] applies to him is not known:

> After a chequered career *De Oude Emigrant* eventually collapsed. The printer, by way of a parting kick tumbling in the heavy thatch roof of the house it was printed in right on the plant, which was completely buried in the debris, and the type hopelessly pi'd. This little job was performed one night. Next morning Potchefstroom knew the vengeful typo no more. He had cleared out to the Orange Free State.

The story would account for the fact that Moll Senior and Borrius were told to put the type in order on 16 December 1861.[3] According to the Potchefstroom correspondent of the Cape Town paper, *Het Volksblad*, it took them two months to tidy up. On 8 April 1862 Borrius was engaged as printer for two years by the Government, and on 24 June 1862 *De Emigrant* (the emigrant) made its first appearance at Potchefstroom, with A. F. Schubart as editor, and Borrius and A. J. Wagner as printers. It survived until 7 October 1862, when one of the warring factions took over the press.

In April 1860 it had been agreed that Pretoria, and not Potchefstroom, was to be the capital city of the country, and on 2 February 1863 Borrius was asked to compile an inventory in readiness for transferring the printing works to Pretoria. It was moved in July 1863, and Pretoria thus became the second place in the Transvaal to have a printing press, excluding missions.

On 18 August 1863 the *Government Gazette* included a Government notice to the effect that the press had moved from Potchefstroom to Pretoria, the new capital of the South African Republic, with C. P. Moll, Junior, as Government Printer. The

1. Nienaber, G. S. *Van Roem tot Selfmoord*. Johannesburg, Voortrekkerpers, 1939, p. 155.
2. 'Looker on P. E.' quoted in *The South African Typographical Journal*, May 1903, p. 9.
3. Vermooten, F. *'n Drukker-pionier: Johannes Philippus Borrius, 1840–1892* ... M A graad in die vak geskiedenis by die Potchefstroomse Universiteitskollege, 1945, [Unpublished], p. 9–21.

younger Moll thus became Pretoria's first printer, and also started Pretoria's first newspaper *De Republikein* (the republican) in May 1864. There is a story that the intention was to publish this journal every week, but because of the shortage of compositors, it had to be published monthly. It did not last long.

When the press moved to Pretoria, Potchefstroom was without a press for a little while, but Borrius had remained there, and when his wife inherited some money in 1866, Borrius bought a house, mortgaged some land to A. Forssman, and obtained an Albion press, with which he started *The Transvaal Argus* on 8 May 1866. It lasted until 11 May 1869, when it became *The Transvaal Advocate*. It was a bilingual weekly, including articles on general subjects, and is today chiefly remembered because the earliest Afrikaans by Transvaal writers occurs in *The Transvaal Argus*. It also included a poem in which the people of the Transvaal were told as early as 1866 to search for gold. Borrius, although not Government Printer, did official printing, such as bank notes in May 1866, and postage stamps from 1870 to 1873. It is said that his wife and children cut the earliest stamps with scissors as they were imperforate. Borrius was not the first to print stamps in the Transvaal. Earlier in the same year some, which are extraordinarily crude and defective, had been printed in Pretoria. M. J. Viljoen, whose name is associated with these poor specimens, was the Treasurer-General, and it is therefore unlikely that he was the printer. Which contractor was it who could not print stamps, or did his apprentices practise on them? Or could they not use the press sent from Germany specially to print stamps?

But to return to Borrius. *The Transvaal Advocate* was followed in 1871(?) by *The Transvaal Advocate and Commercial Advertiser*, which ceased, it is believed, on 16 November 1874. When the Transvaal was annexed by the British in 1877, Borrius lost such work as he had had from the Government, and started a new Dutch weekly paper, *De Transvaal*, on 1 August 1877. It lasted until about August 1881, when it had to cease on account of the war with Britain. Borrius was assisted on this paper and on *The Transvaal Advocate* by Isaac Nicolaas van Alphen, who was born in 1854 in Beek near Nymegen in Holland, and arrived in South Africa at the age of three. In 1866 he entered the printing trade in Pretoria. Dr. Engelenburg[1] tells the story of how Borrius prepared an independence proclamation during the night of 15 and 16 December 1880, and adds that if the Boers had not been victorious Borrius undoubtedly would have been punished for treason. Borrius set the matter, and his assistant, Van Alphen, printed it. Van Alphen entered the Post

1. Combes, P. *Cent Ans de Lutte les Héros Boers, etc.* Paris, Montgredien, [1900?], p. 298.

Office after the War of 1880–81, and became Postmaster-General in 1885. The *Government Gazette* was printed for a short time by Borrius at Potchefstroom, but when the troubles were over, it went back to Pretoria. On 28 February 1883 Borrius started his last, and financially most successful, paper, *De Potchefstroomer*. In 1889 a fire and a slump caused Borrius considerable financial difficulties. When he heard that he had lost a court case, he took carbolic acid, whether by accident or design is not known. He died at Potchefstroom on 3 September 1892, but *De Potchefstroomer* was continued, first by his widow, and into the present century, by his daughter, Mrs. Bischoff, when it was described as a relic of the past. Apparently it was printed on a very old press, and one can but surmise that the press may have been the original Albion Borrius acquired in 1866.

Two of the earliest booklets printed in the Transvaal have survived in the Archives of the Hervormde Kerk (Reformed Church) in Pretoria in the collection brought together by Prof. S. P. Engelbrecht. The one is the Transvaal Constitution (*Grondwet*) printed by Borrius in 1862 in Potchefstroom with an Appendix (*Bylage*) printed by C. P. Moll, Jr., also at Potchefstroom. The other is a volume of regulations for the church (*Reglementen voor de Nederduitsch Hervormde Kerk in de Zuid-Afrikaansche Republiek*), also printed at Potchefstroom in 1862 by Borrius.

It has not been possible to discover when or why Moll Junior ceased to act as contractor to the Government, but some time during the sixties James Cooper Rous undertook to print for the Government. He was born in Cape Town on 20 April 1840, apprenticed to Van de Sandt de Villiers, Tier & Co., and in 1860 or 1861 went first to Natal and then to the Transvaal, where he worked as a clerk in Pretoria.[1] The sources vary about whether it was in 1865, 1867 or 1869 that the Government approached Rous to print for them. After some pressure he agreed, and continued until May 1873, when he sold the remaining term of his contract to J. F. Celliers, but as he shortly afterwards entered into partnership with Celliers, he was connected with Government printing until his death, on 18 June 1876, in Pretoria.

In 1868 Rous and, it is believed, H. Jeppe, started a small newspaper entitled *The Express/De Expresse* in Pretoria. Only volume one, number five for 2 June 1869 is known. Mr. C. J. Frean, Rous's grandson, recorded that his grandfather had difficulty with the Dutch part of the paper, and was assisted by his wife who was a good linguist. When she was unable to help him because of a protracted illness, *The Express* was discontinued.

1. *De Volksstem*, 24 June 1876: In memoriam James Cooper Rous.

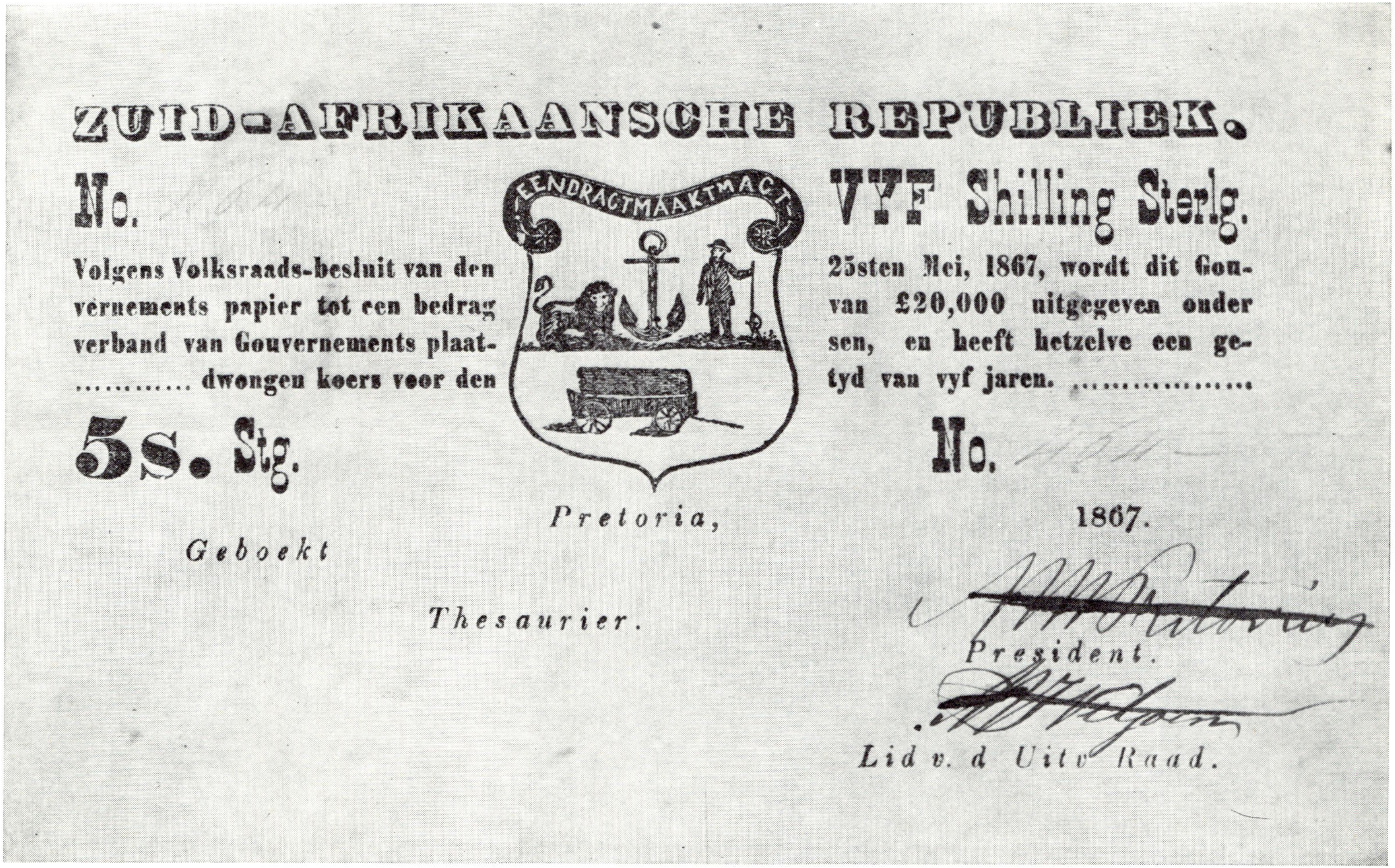

A five-shilling note, printed by Borrius at Pretoria in 1866 or 1867, for the government of the Zuid-Afrikaansche Republiek. The notes were numbered by hand and personally signed. (Approximately natural size.) Original in the Africana Museum, Johannesburg.

Johannes François Celliers was born in Wellington in the Cape Province in 1839, educated in the Paarl, and employed on *Het Volksblad* in Cape Town from 1863, where he was sub-editor in 1872, when President Burgers of the Transvaal approached him to come to Pretoria to start a paper. On arrival in Pretoria in May 1873, Celliers discovered that his plant and material had not arrived, because the ship carrying them had been wrecked between Cape Town and Durban.[1] That was the reason why he joined forces with Rous, and took over the contract for printing the *Government Gazette*. The first issue of the new bilingual weekly, and later very influential, *Volkstem*, appeared on 8 August 1873. It had the financial backing of some important Pretorians, and was printed on one of Moll's old presses. In 1876 the Volksraad decided to tax newspaper advertisements and shortly before his death Rous, and Celliers, as well as the few other Transvaal newspapermen of the time, signed the protest against the tax, which, in the end, was not imposed.

Celliers and Rous also printed a few books, including, perhaps a little unexpectedly, a volume of poetry by the Pretoria businessman Albert Broderick, entitled *Fifty Fugitive Fancies in Verse*, which appeared in 1875.

In 1877 Celliers and *De Volkstem* fell foul of the British who took over the old Government press, but money was collected from the public, and Celliers was able to obtain a new press—'a cylinder machine of American manufacture'.[2] The old press was placed at the disposal of the *Transvaal Argus*.[3] During the siege of Pretoria in the War of 1880–81 the plant of the *Transvaal Argus*, which had started in Pretoria in 1876, was brought to the British camp for security, when the town was evacuated. Permission was obtained by the Editor, C. W. Deecker, and the entertainer, Charles du Val, to use 'the plant, machinery, types, inks, printers, Kaffir steam-power, etc. that went to make up the constituent elements of the Transvaal Thunderer' to produce a newspaper in the camp from 25 February 1880 to 9 April 1881. The press used for most issues of this 'veritable journalistic curiosity', *The News of the Camp*, was none other than Moll's old press. After this last fling, it disappears from history, although it is on record that the *Transvaal Argus* plant was returned to town[4] at the end of the siege.

1. Badenhorst, P. G. *Die Geskiedenis van De Volkstem* 1873–1900: tesis ... M.A. graad by die Universiteit van Suid-Afrika. [1940? Unpublished], p. 8.
2. *The South African Printer and Stationer*, January 1924, p. 517.
3. Behrens, H. P. H. 'The Pretoria Press Story' in *Pretoria (1855–1955); History of the City of Pretoria, etc.* Pretoria, the City Council, 1955, p. 338.
4. Du Val, C. *With a Show through Southern Africa*, ... 2nd ed. London, Tinsley Bros., 1884, p. 159–160.

John Keith is listed as printer and bookseller in Church Street East, Pretoria, in *Jeppe's Almanac* for 1877, and two years later as a member of C. W. Deecker & Co. and the *Transvaal Advertiser*. Deecker had had the contract for printing the *Government Gazette* in English since the British Annexation in 1877 until 1880, when Keith succeeded him. The last issue of this period in English is dated 19 July 1881.

John Keith was responsible for printing one of the most ambitious publications of the Transvaal at this period: a New Testament of 349 pages. The story is told in Darlow and Moule's *Historical Catalogue of the Printed Editions of Holy Scripture in the Library of the British and Foreign Bible Society*. By the end of 1859 various missionaries, including Thomas Morgan Thomas, had established a mission at Inyati among Moselikatse's Matabele in Rhodesia. Just before his death on 8 January 1884, he completed the translation of the New Testament into the Sindebele language. His widow took the manuscript to Pretoria to be printed at her own expense, the cost being £100, but the British and Foreign Bible Society reimbursed her when they came to hear of the story. The edition printed by Keith consisted of 500 copies. Only eighteen had been distributed, when the remainder, which had been stored at a mission station near Inyati, were taken by the Matabele during the Matabele War of 1893–1894 and used as headgear. Small wonder then that little is known of this New Testament with the imprint 'J. Keith, Pretoria, 1884'.

In the same year, on 8 August, Keith started a weekly, *De Republikein* (The Republican). The editor was Jacobus Petrus Toerien (1859–1920), who had been sub-editor of *Di Afrikaanse Patriot* in the Paarl and been sent by the Paarl paper to start something on similar lines in the Transvaal, presumably to popularize the use of Afrikaans instead of Dutch. Only one issue—that of 18 March 1886 in the Library of Parliament, Cape Town, is known.

In 1888 Celliers went into politics, and sold his business to the Government. The *Volkstem* was disposed of to a W. Jonker, and the newspaper, particularly when Dr. F. V. Engelenburg edited it, continued as a power in the land well into the twentieth century. In 1895 it became a daily—the first daily in Dutch in the country, and at much the same time it issued a weekly supplement in French entitled *La Semaine*. The *Volksstem* was also responsible for publishing the first comic paper in the Transvaal, according to the *Cape Argus* of 19 March 1878. It was called *Tsetse*, but nothing more is known of it.

The rest of the staff, plant and equipment which the Government had taken over in 1888, it used to establish a Government Printing Works on 1 August 1888, with P. W. T. Bell as Director and a staff of nineteen. The intention was not only to meet the printing requirements of the state, but also to create employment and to teach young Transvalers the art of printing.

On 14 March 1891 part of the Government Printing Works was destroyed by fire, three machines damaged, and about thirty founts of type destroyed, but worst of all, original documents awaiting binding were a total loss. On 18 March, *The Standard and Diggers' News* of Johannesburg announced that one press had been sufficiently repaired to be fit for printing that week's *Gazette*.

The *Staats Almanak* (State Almanac) of the South African Republic from 1893 to 1899 lists the names of the men employed in specific posts in the Government Printing Works, gives their salaries, and also includes a list of the official publications available from the Staatsdrukkery or Government Printing Office.

In 1896 and 1897 improvements were carried out in the Works, and in 1898 a book of 104 pages of type faces, display types, rules, ornaments, mathematical signs and variations of the Transvaal coat of arms available at the Government Printing Works was published under the title of *Letterproef van de Staatsdrukkery der Zuid-Afrikaansche Republiek, opgericht 1 Augustus 1888.* This is one of the few pre-1900 specimen books issued in South Africa, and may be the only one not in English. The Johannesburg Public Library has a copy. On 15 December 1898 a lithographic section was authorized, but only arrived after the British had taken over in 1900.

When the British, during the war of 1899–1902, sent up twelve printers (known as the 'Twelve Apostles' in the trade) from Natal to man the old Staatsdrukkery, they were impressed by the 'splendidly appointed institution, with everything of the latest pattern pretty well, and the type regulated on the point system'.[1] There were a few grumbles, we are told, because everything was arranged as if the printing works were in Holland.

When the Volksraad of the Orange Free State investigated the possibility of establishing their own Government Printing Works in 1897, it certainly visualized something on the lines of the Staatsdrukkery in Pretoria, but the Free State was at war before anything could be done in the matter. Natal and the Cape continued to put their official printing out to contract until the time of Union in 1910, when the old Staatsdrukkery developed into the Government Printing Works for the whole country.

4. Downes, A. J. *Printers' Saga: being a History of the South African Typographical Union, etc.* Johannesburg, S.A.T.U., 1952, p. 147.

Outside Potchefstroom and Pretoria there was no printing press or newspapers until gold was discovered in the present Pilgrim's Rest area in the early 'seventies. Very little indeed is known about Pilgrim's Rest's first paper. Cutten[1] says the intention was to name it the *Mac-Mac Weekly*, but *The Gold News* was chosen instead. Bulpin[2] records the first issue as appearing on 28 January 1874. It was almost immediately reorganized, and in February *The Goldfields Mercury* appeared in its place. The editor was an Irishman, M. V. Phelan, who had a number of skirmishes with the authorities because of the impolitic things in his paper. Theal[3] records that it ceased to appear after April 1878. Where Phelan's press came from or whether he was a real printer, or, indeed, even whether his paper was actually printed at Pilgrim's Rest, has not been discovered.

The first paper in Barberton, where gold was found in 1884, is *The Barberton Herald and Transvaal Mining Mail* established on 4 May 1886, with Gordon Cameron as editor and Eaton & Bold as publishers. Nothing has been found about any of these men, but there is a possibility that the last named is the same John Southwold Bold who lived in Pretoria, according to the *Transvaal Almanacs*, from 1877 to 1881. But was he also the J. S. Bold of the *Cradock News* and its Dutch counterpart who published the first book in Afrikaans by L. H. Meurant in 1861?

The following taken over by *The Weekly Mail* from the *Glasgow Evening Times* of 12 February 1887 is quoted in full, as it gives a vivid picture of journalism in the Transvaal at the time:

We have received from South Africa a curiosity in journalism. It is a copy of the 'Barberton Herald and Transvaal Mining Mail', of Tuesday, January 4, published at Barberton, De Kaap, Transvaal. What the 'Barberton Herald' may be like on ordinary occasions we do not know, but the appearance of this particular number is decidedly interesting. It consists of three small sheets of various sizes. Two of these are blue and one white, and the paper has evidently been intended for commercial purposes, as it is ruled with blue and red lines. How this delightful variety occurs is explained by the editor in a leading article headed 'Ourselves'. Barberton, though making great strides in the march of progress, has not yet been supplied with a paper manufactory, and it is far from the base of supplies. 'It is just possible,' the editor remarks, 'that our readers may have noticed that occasionally our issue is somewhat variegated in colour, and oft-times is printed on foolscap, and more rarely on blotting-paper. Now, that is really not our own fault, for our

1. Cutten, T. E. G. *A History of the Press in South Africa, etc.* Cape Town, National Union of South African Students, 1935, p. 56.
2. Bulpin, T. V. *Lost Trails on the Low Veld, etc.* Cape Town, Howard B. Timmins for Hodder & Stoughton, [1950?], p. 125–126.
3. Theal, G. M. *History of South Africa from 1873 to 1884, etc.* London, George Allen & Unwin, (1919), vol. 1, p. 297.

ordinary printing paper has been a considerable time on the road, and its non-arrival must be attributed to the "shoot", bad roads, inclement weather, scarcity of transport, and the acts of Providence generally.'

A NEIGHBOURLY TURN

But the 'Barberton Herald' has a neighbour, the 'Gold Fields Times', and they occasionally do each other a friendly turn. The former has lately borrowed three reams of paper, and the latter has now and again received in loan the 'galley press'. The 'Herald's' paper not arriving in time for the last publication of 1885, the proprietors were in desperate straits, and sent their agents to 'The Times' to ask in dulcet tones to be favoured with another loan. This was refused, 'and now,' says the editor, 'our respective staffs are not even on speaking terms.' The 'Times', however, soon found it necessary to ask again for the loan of its contemporary's galley press, but 'our foreman being well acquainted with the selfish spirit displayed by the "Times", declined any further interchange of civilities'. Then followed a declaration of war. The 'Times' sent its contemporary a claim for £5. 5s., the price of three reams of paper, and for a further sum of £150 'being damage and loss sustained through your failing to return the abovementioned paper within the time promised thus causing my clients a week's delay in issuing their paper'. This claim was to be met at once, on pain of legal proceedings.

PUERILE IMBECILITY

The 'Herald' considered, 'the tenor of this letter to be nothing but an outburst of puerile imbecility, its silliness being only equalled by its cheek', and sent a counter claim showing a balance of two shillings in its favour. It welcomes the threatened legal proceedings, with 'possible joy', and concludes with the announcement to its many readers that its new plant, 'one of the finest north of the Orange River', will positively arrive within a month, when it will have plenty of scope to ventilate grievances and give reliable mining information. Such are some of the incidents which give variety to colonial newspaper life.

The story was continued by E. L. Williams, the Editor of the *Barberton Herald*, to the *Weekly Mail* as follows under the heading 'Brown Sugar Paper':

In your issue of the 4th of May, 1887, sent me by some friends from Barry, you refer to a dispute about three reams of paper which occurred between a contemporary and ourselves. I am glad to say that the dispute was settled very satisfactorily by our rendering an account covering the amount claimed. The press in this distant part is conducted with some difficulty. We are nearly 500 miles from the nearest Natal railway station, and owing to the great difficulties of transport at the time to which reference was made, we were printing our 'Herald' on blotting paper, a copy of which I post you today. In December last year we were in such straits that we were constrained to try brown sugar paper, but, dry, it would not take the ink, and wet, it broke. This was the night of publication, but the Cape mail, via Pretoria, was to arrive, and it brought us two reams of double demy, which carried us through for another week; our new plant arrived a week after, with a good supply.

Later A. W. Bayly printed the *Barberton Herald* and the *Gold Fields News*, but more ambitious is the local almanac known as *De Kaap Annual* which he compiled and printed annually from about 1894 to 1899. It contains particulars about the mines, many statistics, and a Barberton directory and is one of the small number of substantial works printed by a country press in the Transvaal.

By the middle of 1886 it was known that there was payable gold on the Witwatersrand, and by the end of the year Johannesburg had been established. The discovery of these gold fields changed everything, including printing and publishing, not only in the Transvaal, but in the whole of South Africa. The *Volkstem*, as early as 14 September 1886 reported that the first journalist to visit the Witwatersrand was D. F. du Toit, Editor of the *Patriot* (Paarl), followed by C. Borckenhagen of the *Express* (Bloemfontein), and F. Dormer of the Argus (Cape Town).

Small wonder then that on 10 December 1886 the *Volkstem*, quoting the *Transvaal Advertiser*, reported that the *Republikein* of Pretoria 'intends removing its office to Witwatersrand shortly, with the view to enlighten the diggers there as to the mysteries of patriotism, and for the spread of 'onze taal' [our language] and the peculiar politics of its Paarl contemporary'.[1] This note from a contemporary newspaper, no doubt, elucidates the following statement by Hedley A. Chilvers, which has puzzled students of the press in Johannesburg: 'Johannesburg's first newspaper was a Dutch journal published by a certain Du Toit. Its life was brief, and even its name has been forgotten.'[2]

All doubt, however, is removed by the article of 'A Pioneer Pressman' (whose identity unfortunately has not been discovered) in the *Rand Daily Mail* of 22 September 1906 to mark the twentieth anniversary of the birth of Johannesburg. He, in writing about 'The Fourth Estate: Reminiscences of the Early Days. Notable Journals and Journalists', referred to the British delight in newspapers, and continued: 'it will come as somewhat of a surprise to know that despite those efforts, [to establish a newspaper] the first real newspaper sheet which was published was in Dutch. This was a journal printed and published by Mr. du Toit (a connexion of the celebrated Rev. S. du Toit of the Africander Bond) in January, 1887.' It was a weekly, mainly concerned with local affairs and included, according to 'A Pioneer Pressman' English translations of important Government notices. On 13 December 1887, when a commission had to report on the advisability of publishing Govern-

1. This reference was kindly supplied by the late Mr. S. A. Rochlin.
2. Chilvers, H. A. *Out of the Crucible: being the Romantic Story of the Witwatersrand Goldfields; and of the Great City which arose in their midst, etc.* London, Cassell, (1929), p. 249.

A Christmas card from the staff of the Transvaal Mining Argus *printed in honour of their employer and his*
(Approximately natural size.) Original in the Africana Museum, Johannes

Compliments of the Season.

WE, THE STAFF OF THE

"TRANSVAAL MINING ARGUS,"

Take the opportunity afforded by this occasion of wishing

MR. AND MRS. DEECKER

A

MERRY CHRISTMASTIDE,

And of expressing to them our sincere and heartfelt wishes for the coming year.

We are fully aware, Sir, of the exceptional difficulties with which you have had to contend, in order to render your paper a financial as well as a literary success. Severe competition and extreme local depression have retarded to no inconsiderable extent the onward progress and growth of your enterprise, but we are glad to say that withal these unavoidable "contretemps" the name and reputation of what is undoubtedly THE paper in this mining centre have been sustained and preserved satisfactorily; in fact we may say favourably.—We would furthermore assure you, that it is our wish, and it shall be our aim, to devote our joint interests to your benefit and advantage, in the earnest hope that your publication may in time to come rank amongst the foremost daily productions in South Africa.—Permit us, Sir, again to thank you for your constant kindness and consideration and to wish you

A Happy New Year.

ment notices in Johannesburg papers, it was said that this paper had a very small circulation and was inaccurate.[1] On 2 February 1888 the *Eastern Star* reported that the *Republikein* would shortly be discontinued and that the printing plant was on offer to several newspaper proprietors. It was, however, still appearing by the end of February 1888, but as no more is heard of it, the assumption is that it closed down soon after. Two items bearing the imprint of the *Republikein* or *Republican* in Johannesburg, are both dated 1887, and are a pamphlet relating to Nellmapius and another of the articles of association of an early Transvaal gold company, the Nabob.

On 6 February 1887 Will Crosby's printing plant arrived in Johannesburg,[2] and Fred. R. Lovegrove and Henry Wright[3] produced *The Diggers' News and Witwatersrand Advertiser* on 24 February 1887, of which a copy can be seen in the Africana Museum, Johannesburg, where there is also the first issue of *The Transvaal Mining Argus* which appeared on 25 February 1887. As the latter was for a time printed in Pretoria by J. Keith for circulation on the gold fields, it is not a Johannesburg publication in the same way as Du Toit or Crosby's papers. The story goes that Crosby's firm was asked to print a dodger announcing the publication of *The Transvaal Mining Argus* by C. W. Deecker of Pretoria, and that Crosby's was therefore able to forestall Deecker. When its plant arrived towards the end of 1887, *The Transvaal Mining Argus* became Johannesburg's first daily—an honour one does not begrudge it. It ceased publication towards the end of September 1893; and *The Diggers' News* was amalgamated in 1890 with *The Standard and Transvaal Mining Chronicle*, which had started on 12 March 1887. They became the *Standard and Diggers' News*, which survived until the British took Johannesburg in 1900, commandered the plant, and used it from 2 June 1900 to print the military organ, *The Johannesburg Gazette*, in which all military notices appeared. Later the plant went to the *Rand Daily Mail*,[4] and there is an account of how the Linotype machines were dismantled in 1926,[5] after having seen service since 1899.

The Standard and Diggers' News was said to be subsidised by the Kruger Government and was not popular with the English-speaking or 'Uitlander' group in Johannesburg, but it was well edited and more venturesome than most of its con-

1. Gray, J. *Payable Gold, etc.* South Africa, Central News Agency, 1937, p. 212.
2. Rosenthal, E. 'Early Johannesburg Printers and Publishers' in *Africana Notes and News*, August 1944, p. 15, and Gray, J. *Payable Gold etc.* South Africa, Central New Agency, 1937.
3. Lovegrove, *Mrs.* A. 'Johannesburg's First Newspaper' in *Rand Daily Mail*, 3 October 1936.
4. Bell, W. H. S. *Bygone Days, etc.* London, H. & F. Witherby, (1933), p. 137.
5. *The South African Printer and Stationer*, January 1927, p. 15.

temporaries, making provision (when this was not the custom) to get an early edition available in Pretoria, and to issue a special London edition.

In celebrating the twelfth anniversary of the establishment of the forerunners of this paper, G. A. Allwright recalled how he and a Mr. Richter produced the first issue with composing sticks made by a local carpenter, as their own had been lost on the way up from Port Elizabeth. It is also on record that the press was a Columbian and that there was just sufficient type for four pages. Their office was a tent.[1] Henry Wright, then Editor of *The Standard*, presided at the first Johannesburg Wayzgoose held at Halfway House at Christmas 1889.[2] The London journal, *South Africa* of 23 February 1889 reported that 'South Africa is just now an El Dorado for printers, and there is room probably for a few hundreds of them. The new Gold Fields have drained the lower colonies of editors, reporters, compositors, machine hands, and the whole body corporate of a newspaper office. The comps and machine minders are getting fabulous wages, £4 to £8 a week being the average. Steady men are certain of work and high pay. Master printers just now are not competing so much for jobs as for good hands. Most of the offices are choked with jobbing.' Much of this 'jobbing' was required by the numerous mining companies started all over the place, and some of Johannesburg's earliest surviving examples of printing during the first five or six years of its existence are to be found among collections of old scrip, share certificates, company prospectuses and reports. The printers in most cases were the newspaper presses, but firms, such as Lovegrove & Co., W. E. Burmester, and Wood & Hockey, undertook printing of all kinds together with journalism, advertising, bookbinding, and whatever else came along it seems. An early example of this type of work is the twenty-seven page pamphlet *Witwatersrand, Johannesburg, and other Gold Fields*, by Charles Cowen, dated Johannesburg, December 1887, printed by T. & G. Sheffield.

Thomas and George Sheffield were the founders of *The Star*, the only Johannesburg pioneer newspaper still in existence and one of the most important in South Africa. The full story is told in *Today's News Today: the Story of the Argus Company*, published in November 1956 to commemorate the centenary of the *Cape Argus*, one of the other influential papers in this group.

1. Cutten, T. E. G. *A History of the Press in South Africa, etc.* Cape Town, National Union of South African Students, 1935, p. 58–59.
2. Downes, A. J. *Printers' Saga: being a History of the South African Typographical Union, etc.* Johannesburg, S.A.T.U., 1952, p. 19.

Thomas and George Sheffield had come to the Cape in 1860, and by 1885 they were publishing the *Eastern Star* in Grahamstown. In July 1887 Thomas Sheffield went to see Johannesburg for himself and on 16 September 1887 they announced that the *Eastern Star* would, from October, appear in Johannesburg. They moved their entire plant by rail as far as Kimberley, and the remaining three hundred miles, by ox wagon, as Johannesburg was not connected by rail to the Cape until 15 September 1892. On 17 October 1887 the *Eastern Star* appeared in Johannesburg continuing its numbering from Grahamstown. The printing works, stationery shop, and the general store were the responsibility of George Sheffield, while his brother looked after the editorial side. On 29 March 1889, when the Sheffields and F. J. Dormer joined forces and established the Argus Printing and Publishing Company, the name of the paper was changed from *Eastern Star* to *The Star*. The story of *The Star* is to a great extent the story of Johannesburg and of South Africa. It might perhaps be of interest to quote what must be a very early Johannesburg advertisement for *The Star*. It appeared in Johannesburg's first *Directory* issued by Turner with a preface dated January 1889—just over two years after the first farms were proclaimed public diggings:

> 'The Eastern Star'
> Published every
> Monday, Wednesday and Friday afternoons
> by
> T. & G. Sheffield,
> Jhb
> Contains the most complete mining information and
> has the largest circulation on Witwatersrand, and the
> Cape Colony, Free State and Natal.
> Printing of all kinds
> Executed with promptitude and care.
> T & G. Sheffield,
> President Street,
> Johannesburg

Except for jobbing printing, *The Star* of today may very well make the same claims.

The Star was not the first afternoon paper in Johannesburg. This honour goes to the *Daily News*, which was published every evening by Josias Angove. He had started the *Vryburg Advocate*, 'but the quiescent state of the country and the counter-attractions of the Transvaal goldfields induced him to remove his plant thither in

1887.' The story goes that in crossing the Vaal River, his wagon overturned, and much of his printing plant was lost.

On 18 October 1887 the *Volkstem* noted that it had the previous week received the first four numbers of the *Daily News* and continued: 'We wish our contemporary every success but cannot help thinking that journalism is being just a little bit overdone at the Rand,' and one might add, all through the 'eighties and 'nineties. The Weekly Edition of *The Standard and Diggers' News* of 7 January 1899 lists seven papers which had 'succumbed in 1898' and two which had reduced their frequency, and most of them were on the Rand.

One of the earliest publications of a more literary nature than company reports and the like to be printed in Johannesburg is Sir Percy FitzPatrick's *Through Mashonaland with Pick and Pen*. The letters from Rhodesia first appeared in *The Star*, and were so popular, that the Argus Printing and Publishing Co. issued them separately in 1892 with a locally lithographed cover. This is today an extremely rare item, but whether it really is the first book published in Johannesburg cannot be said with any certainty, as it may have had a predecessor of which no copies or records have survived. To the Argus Company also goes the honour of printing the first Johannesburg, and for that matter, South African, magazine intended for women, called *The Ladies Magazine*, which was published monthly from October 1894 until March 1895. Before Johannesburg was all of ten years old papers in foreign languages, such as Yiddish and German, were being printed, as well as legal, commercial, scientific and other specialized journals (among these *The South African Mining Journal* of today, which started in 1892), sporting and hobbies magazines, and of course humorous and satirical journals, which made their appearance as early as 21 February 1888 in Johannesburg when 'Baron' Gluckstein started the *Bulletin*. Apparently this early paper had some trouble with its printing for the *Standard* of 17 March 1888 noted: 'The *Bulletin* requested the *Standard* to offer some apologies for the miserable appearance which their sheet would present. We do apologise ... as we feel there is much need to, neither is it beautiful to the eye nor commendable to anyone's common sense.'

After 1886 various country towns in the Transvaal were establishing printing presses. Dr. Gustav Preller published a chronological list of the oldest newspapers in Natal, the Orange Free State, and the Transvaal[1] in which he listed *The Transvaal* as appear-

1. *De Volkstem*, 1 October 1924, p. 11.

ing in Lydenburg on 29 November 1887. John H. Parker, Lynch & Co., and P. Joubert & Co. are names associated with this English weekly, which apparently continued until the end of September 1899. In an advertisement which appeared in 1895, when P. Joubert & Co. were the owners,[1] it is stated that *The Transvaal* is the only paper in the district of Lydenburg and 'all kinds of Job Printing executed'.

Klerksdorp was the next place to have a press—once again a mining area. The *Klerksdorp Pioneer* was announced on 1 August 1888 by the *Volkstem* of 20 July 1888, but Dr. Preller records its starting date as 23 July. As no copies seem to be available in any public collection in South Africa, it is impossible to state exactly when Klerksdorp had its first newspaper. By 21 November 1888 George Vickers had started *The Klerksdorp Representative* which H. M. Guest took over in 1889, and changed to *The Klerksdorp Mining Record* on 24 August 1889. Here once again, the difficulties under which printers had to work before 1900 are clear. The issue of *The Klerksdorp Mining Record* for 12 March 1890 is printed on wrapping paper, because, owing to heavy rains, the roads between Klerksdorp and the railhead at Kimberley were impassable and all supplies were late, including paper for the newspaper.

Steynsdorp in the Eastern Transvaal was the centre of the Komati Goldfield in 1887, when the Scotsman, George Adamson, arrived from Natal, where he had been on the *Times of Natal*, and started *Komati Observer* the next year. Although Adamson had left with his plant by 1892, *The Critic* of 29 June 1894 still referred to the *Komati Observer*, which, one can but assume, must have been resuscitated.

Pietersburg, the most important town in the Zoutpansberg in the Northern Transvaal had a press by November 1888. The press may actually have started at Smitsdorp, fifteen miles away, as the London journal, *South Africa* of 4 January 1889 and *Jeppe's Transvaal Almanac* for 1889, both note the *Zoutpansberg Mining Journal* as being issued at this place. It was founded by no less a person than F. H. Hamilton, editor of *The Star* in 1894–96. *South Africa* noted that this was the northernmost site of a printing press and a newspaper in South Africa at the time and that the journal was 'nicely printed'. In 1890 the local paper was called *The Zoutpansberg Review*, which must be a continuation of the earlier paper, as it gives 1888 as the year it was established[2]. Its Dutch counterpart was the *Zoutpansberg Wachter* established in August 1896.

1. Mitchell & Co., C. *The Newspaper Press Directory and Advertisers' Guide*, 1895, p. 186.
2. *Ratcliffe's Guide to the South African Press, 1902–3*. London, Ratcliffe, Dunbar, 1902.

One of the editors of one of these papers in the early days is on record[1] as having drunk so much that his paper appeared at irregular intervals instead of weekly—a typical occurrence in the nineteenth century among printers and newspaper men in many parts of the country.

Krugersdorp and Nylstroom both had newspapers for the first time in 1893. Krugersdorp's *Vierkleur*, edited by General Ben Viljoen, does not appear to have survived, and it is not known in which month it started. Krugersdorp, however, in common with a few other South African and Rhodesian towns started off with handwritten or cyclostyled newspapers before the advent of a printing press. The Johannesburg paper, *Standard*, of 14 March 1888 recorded the establishment of a 'modest little illustrated sheet published locally' in Krugersdorp. It was called the *Krugersdorp Burster*, and what particularly impressed the Johannesburg journalist was the excellence of the illustrations in pen and ink which 'betray the hand of an experienced and accomplished artist'. Unfortunately the artist's name has not been recorded.

The Nylstroom paper, *De Boerenvriend* (the farmer's friend) is reported by *The Critic* (Johannesburg) of 14 July 1893 to have started at the beginning of the month, but Dr. Preller noted it as appearing on 22 June 1893. The *Staats-almanak* of the second half of the last decade of the nineteenth century recorded J. R. Reynolds as editor, but he also occurs as publisher in contemporary sources, and may even have been the printer. In August 1897 the paper was moved from Nylstroom to Pietersburg. There are at least five variant forms of the title.

Boksburg and Springs, both important centres on the Reef, had newspapers, and presumably a printing press, by 1895, while more distant places such as Ermelo and Heidelberg were not far behind. *The Middelburg Courant: District and High Veldt Gazette* started on 1 January 1895 and cost sixpence. Mr. O. H. Frewin, who was a Transvaal expert on print, reported that he had seen a cutting from the *Middelburg Courant* dating from about 1898, and that it resembled a missing word competition. He surmised that the type had been supplied from a Thorne Type Composing Machine. *The Critic* of 11 January 1895 in welcoming the new paper, stated that 'the railway expansion in the Transvaal is responsible for this publication, which is issued in English and Dutch'—the usual practice in most country papers, and even sometimes in the bigger centres, to attract more readers in a bilingual community.

1. Munnik, G. G. *Kronieke van Noordelike Transvaal, etc.* Pretoria, Suid-Afrikaanse Boekwinkel, [1926?] p. 92.

To find anything other than newspapers printed by these country presses is extremely difficult, as their jobbing work was generally speaking of a very ephemeral nature—dodgers, official and other blanks, account forms, and an occasional programme. Moreover, much of the little which has survived, carries no printer's name or place of printing, and no date. Until the railway came to the Transvaal, the difficulty and expense of transporting plant and materials discouraged any but the most venturesome from setting up a press. But even after many of the transportation problems had been overcome, the high wages required, made printing in the Transvaal far more expensive than elsewhere. Until the discovery of gold, and the consequent influx of people, the demand for products of the printing press was extremely small and was largely satisfied by importing from Holland and Britain. To encourage local Transvaal printing, it was decided to charge 100% import duty on foreign printing in 1892. In March 1893 it is recorded that £45 worth of printed matter was imported from Europe, and £53 from the Cape and Natal.

As the history of printing in any country is bound up with the liberty of the press, reference must here be made briefly to the position in the Transvaal.

The Grondwet or Constitution as published in the *Government Gazette* of 5 March 1858 allowed the press its freedom, but stipulated that publisher and printer were held responsible for any libel in the newspaper. Law No. 3 of 1881 required a statement from the owner and the printer concerning the proper name of the paper, its address, as well as the name and address of the owner and the printer. The names of the printer and publisher had to be printed on each issue of the paper. Printed matter such as books and pamphlets were also to carry the name and address of the printer. A similar law was promulgated on 25 February 1885. In 1896 Law No. 26 required the press to comply with certain conditions, such as giving the names of the writers of certain articles. It also gave the State President the right, with the advice and consent of the Executive Council, to prohibit the circulation of printed or published matter, the contents of which he considered to be in conflict with good morals, or dangerous to peace and order in the country.

When feelings were beginning to run high in Johannesburg during the 'nineties, some of the newspapers were certainly outspoken in their criticism of the Government. The first to come under the axe was *The Critic*, which was founded in 1891 as a weekly. It was involved in various law suits, and the editor, Henry Hess, considered it wiser to go to England to start *The African Critic*, while the Johannesburg paper continued in his absence. The latter was suspended for six months on 18

December 1896. *The Star* was suspended on 24 March 1897 for three months. Apparently the Government's intention was known and the warrant not entirely unsuspected. So the necessary arrangements had been made for *The Comet* to appear in place of *The Star* on 25 March 1897. The matter was taken to the Supreme Court, and judgment was given for publishers of *The Star*. On the day after the judgment, 15 April 1897, *The Star* once again appeared. Law No. 14 of 1898 repealed some of the offending clauses in the law of 1896, and the press was freed from various disabilities.

It was not only Kruger's government that tried to muzzle a hostile press. The *Volkstem's* editorial staff had suffered in 1880 when the British were in occupation in the Transvaal.

As the earliest printing presses brought to the Transvaal before 1892 had to be brought at least three hundred miles by ox wagon, and in nearly every case had been used elsewhere in South Africa, the assumption is that they were both small, and, in many cases, obsolete models. The story of the printing plant used by *The Star* will serve to illustrate what happened in many instances.

R. W. Murray established *The Great Eastern* in Grahamstown towards the end of 1863, where it was the first Eastern Province newspaper to be printed by steam. By 1868 it had ceased publication, and the plant was acquired by J. V. O'Brien who used it mainly for jobbing work, but also printed the *Grahamstown Advertiser* and *Anglo-African*, which became the *Eastern Star* on 1 January 1871. The Sheffields took over the printing works, used it in Grahamstown for a while, and brought their plant to Johannesburg to start *The Star* on 17 October 1887. It is on record that they needed three wagons to bring up the press, the boiler and steam engine.[1]

The Editor of *The Potchefstroom Herald* stated on 21 November 1957 that the Wharfedale printing press used to print his paper when it started in 1908 was the original machine brought up from Grahamstown by the Sheffield Brothers when they launched *The Star* in Johannesburg. Cutten[2] states that when Johannesburg celebrated its fortieth anniversary '*The Star* had a float in the procession on which was the first printing press of any magnitude ever used in Johannesburg, that brought by the Sheffield brothers from Grahamstown'. If these traditions are correct,

1. *Today's News Today: the story of the Argus Company*. Johannesburg, Argus Printing & Publishing Co., (1956), p. 36.
2. Cutten, T. E. G. *A History of the Press in South Africa, etc.* Cape Town, National Union of South African Students, 1935, p. 60.

Front and reverse of the medal of honour awarded too the Government Printing Office of the Zuid-Afrika[illegible] Republiek at the Paris World Fair, 1900. (Actual size.) Original in the Africana Museum, Johanne[illegible]

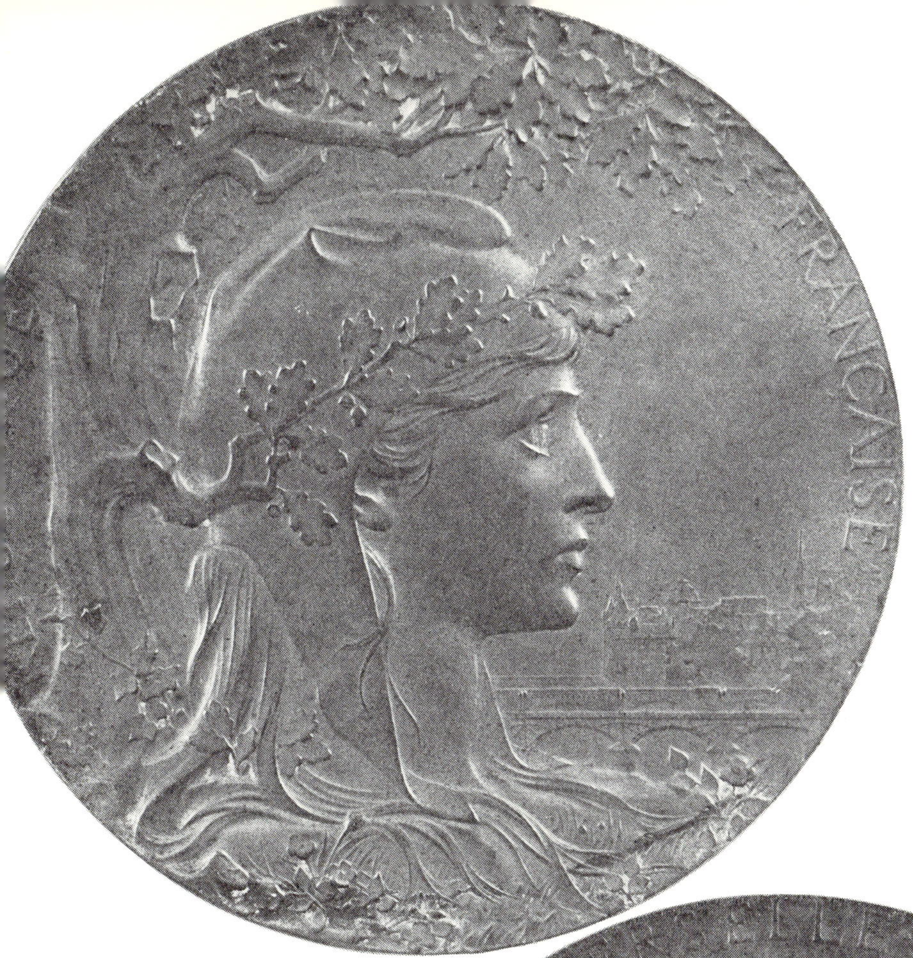
FRANÇAISE

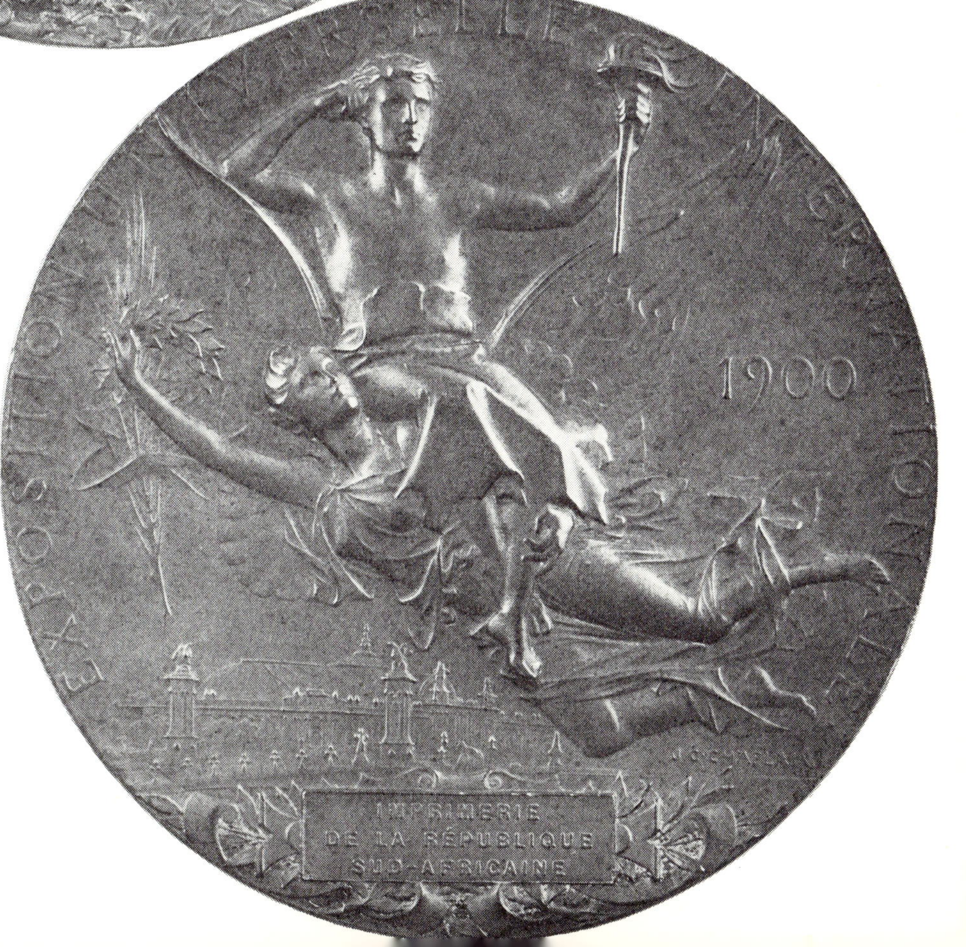
1900
IMPRIMERIE
DE LA RÉPUBLIQUE
SUD-AFRICAINE

the new machinery—including 'a printing machine with the latest folding attachment and a powerful steam engine'—which had been ordered by 29 March 1889, must have arrived before 25 May 1890, when *The Star* Works were destroyed by fire. The losses included machines for letterpress and lithography. But *The Star* did not miss an issue. The Managing Director, F. J. Dormer, almost overnight bought the plant of the *Golden Age*, which was for sale for £3,500, and a little later added the entire plant of the *Goldfields Times*, which had come from Barberton to Johannesburg, where it ceased publication after three months. Orders were sent overseas by *The Star* for two feeder Wharfedale folders, a machine for lithography, 50 column galleys, 20 double column galleys, 10 frames, 100 pairs of cases and other equipment.[1]

By the end of 1893 a Cox-Duplex Rotary had been imported—the first in the country.[2] By June 1897 stereotyped plates were in use on a rotary machine which could produce 20,000 to 24,000 copies an hour.[3] On 2 April 1898 *The Star* introduced Linotypes from Canada—the first paper in South Africa to dispense with composing by hand—and gave a party to celebrate the occasion.[4] A Pretoria paper, possibly *The Press*, is said to have had a Thorne type-setting machine in 1895, but presumably did not find it sufficiently satisfactory to be able to do away with hand-setting.

Just before the outbreak of the South African War in October 1899, similar improvements in plant were being made in the bigger centres throughout South Africa, and with the growth of the population, the increase in wealth occasioned by the greater output of the mines, and the improvement in all types of communication, the demand for print was far more insistent, though the emphasis was still on newspaper and jobbing printing. Very little, if any, really good typography was produced, and book-printing as such had to wait for the twentieth century.

1. *Today's News Today: the story of the Argus Company*. Johannesburg, Argus Printing & Publishing Co., (1956), p. 54–55.
2. *The Star*, 18 October 1937.
3. *Today's News Today: the story of the Argus Company*. Johannesburg, Argus Printing & Publishing Co., (1956), p. 108.
4. *Standard and Diggers' News*, 6 April 1898, p. 4.

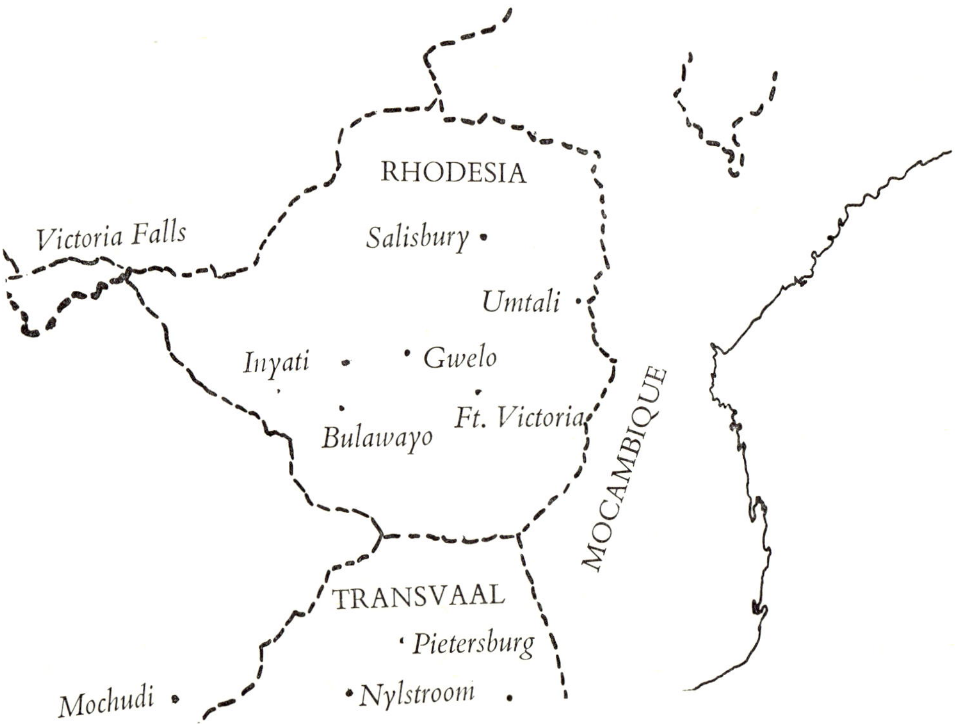
RHODESIA
Victoria Falls
Salisbury
Umtali
Inyati
Gwelo
Ft. Victoria
Bulawayo
MOCAMBIQUE
TRANSVAAL
Pietersburg
Mochudi
Nylstroom

The Beginnings of Printing in Adjacent Territories

In October 1889 Rhodes obtained a Royal Charter for the British South Africa Company; on 27 June 1890 the Pioneer Column began its march into Mashonaland; and on 12 September 1890, Fort Salisbury came into being.

As the country north of the Limpopo River was being opened up, the printing press slowly found its way farther northward. The first piece of real printing (not cyclostyling) produced north of the Limpopo River was a four-page paper entitled *News and Advertisements* published in Salisbury on 17 September 1893 'pending completion of arrangements for the printing of the forthcoming *Rhodesia Herald*'.[1] As all the printing materials had not yet arrived in Salisbury, the printer had to apologize for not putting 'Mr.' before the names of gentlemen riders, because he did not have sufficient quantity of type of the letter M.

In Bulawayo printing of *The Bulawayo Chronicle* started on 12 October 1894 with plant sent up from Johannesburg.[2]

Umtali had its first printed newspaper, *The Rhodesia Advertiser*, in August 1895.[3]

On 4 November 1897 the railway between Mafeking and Bulawayo was completed and this was the occasion when brochures were printed by the jobbing section of the *Bulawayo Chronicle*.[4]

Gwelo and Fort Victoria also had newspapers, and one assumes printing presses, during the next few years.

First the Rebellions and then the South African War, made it impossible for the sparsely populated Rhodesia to do much in the way of printing before the end of

1. *The Rhodesian Press: the History of the Rhodesian Printing and Publishing Company Ltd.* Salisbury, Rhodesian Printing & Publishing Co., (1962), p. 16.
2. *Ibidem*, p. 24.
3. *Ibidem*, p. 40.
4. *Ibidem*, p. 51.

NEWS AND ADVERTISEMENTS

Issued pending completion of arrangements for the printing of the forthcoming "Rhodesia Herald."

SALISBURY, SATURDAY, SEPTEMBER 17TH, 1892. PRICE 6

PUBLISHERS' NOTICE.

In bringing out this little sheet of news and advertisements—the very first matter ever printed in Mashonaland—the publishers ask the public to bear in mind the fact that only a portion of the plant, type, and material of the "Rhodesia Herald" is as yet to hand, and that the first issue of that long and ardently awaited newspaper will not appear for several weeks to come. It is to meet in some degree the urgent demand for a medium of news and notices, and especially to put briefly on record the leading events of a particularly eventful week, that the present effort has been determined on.

TELEGRAMS.

Johannesburg, Sept. 10th, Special.—August output: 102,322 ozs.

Johannesburg, Sept. 10th. Special.—Kimberley Exhibition was opened on Thursday by Governor Loch in great pomp and in the presence of 2,000 people. Attendance has been large up to the present.

MASHONALAND TURF CLUB

Spring Meeting, September 12th and 14th.

On Monday and Wednesday last the Sprin[g] Meeting of the Club came off in good b[ut] hazy weather. The racecourse presented a[n] animated appearance throughout the time, an[d] there was a pleasing array of ladies. Su[b]joined are brief notices of the events, includi[ng] Tuesday's sports :—

1. TRIAL PLATE.—Value 50 sovs. F[or] horses that have never won more th[an] £40 advertised value. £4. Weight f[or] age. Allowed 7 lbs. 6 furlongs.

C. H. Zeederberg's Cowl, 9-5, Ballantyne
A. E. Burnett's Saraband, 9-5, ... Cowan
H. J. Borrow's Unknown, 9-5 (carried 11-5) ... ... Hay

Betting: 2 to 1 on Cowl; 5 to 1 again[st] Unknown; 2 to 1 against Saraband W[on] easily by Cowl in the commonest of canters.

2. PONY RACE.—Value 10 sovs. For pon[ies] 14 hands and under. Entrance, £[...] Catch weights, not under 10 st. Distan[ce] half a mile.

H. J. Borrow's Honest ... Cowan
W. L. Cornwall's Sportsman ... Chappe
Mr. Wybergh's William ... Nunn
Mr. Savile's Punch ... Ballantyne

Betting: 3 to 1 on Honest; 3 to 1 again[st] Sportsman; any price the others. Mr. Bo[r]row's Honest led from the start, and ne[ver] gave her backers any doubt, winning by ab[out] five lengths.

the century, and even mission presses had not been established between the Limpopo and the Zambezi Rivers.

Although South-West Africa was known to hunters and explorers in the very early days, the first white men to settle there were missionaries in the nineteenth century. Others followed. In 1863 when the native peoples of the territory were at war with each other, the missionaries asked for German protection, and in 1884 a German Protectorate was declared.

Apart from mission presses, the earliest place in South-West Africa to have a newspaper is Windhoek. The *Windhuker Anzeiger* was established in Windhoek in 1898 by the *Rechtsanwalt* Wasserfall, and was not only the first paper in South-West Africa, but indeed in any of the old German Colonies. Before the outbreak of World War I it became the *Deutsch-Südwest Afrikanische Zeitung*, and was published twice a week.[1] The assumption is that a press must have been available in South-West Africa at this date. Although there are some publications relating to South-West Africa written by Colonists, they all seem to have been printed outside the territory, if not by a mission press.

Angola, on the west coast of Africa to the north of South-West Africa, was explored between 1482 and 1485 by Diogo Cam, and has been Portuguese territory ever since except for the period 1641–1648, when the Dutch were there. Loanda, was founded in 1575, and, according to Henry Cotton, 'the only specimen of its typography which I have heard of is *Two Catechisms in Aethiopic*, edited by Franc. Paccone, for the use of converted natives, printed in 1641 (Fabrii Lux Sal. Evang.)'.[2] If Cotton is correct in this statement, and if this work was really printed in Loanda in 1641, to Angola and not to Mauritius or the Cape goes the honour of being the first to print in the Southern hemisphere. Unfortunately Cotton is at fault, as these Catechisms were specially printed in Europe for use in Angola.

The southern part of Moçambique (or Mozambique), also known as Portuguese East Africa, is to the east of the Transvaal and Rhodesia, and has been in contact with the Portuguese since the early years of the sixteenth century. Until the nineteenth century the country itself was in a constant state of unrest, and printing did not

1. Schnee, H. *Deutsches Kolonial-Lexikon*, Leipzig, Quelle & Meyer, (1920), vol. 3, p. 100.
2. Cotton, H. *A Typographical Gazetteer attempted ... 2nd series*. Oxford, Clarendon Press, 1866, p. 123.

e first piece of printing ever done in Rhodesia.
ghtly reduced.) Original in the Johannesburg Public Library.

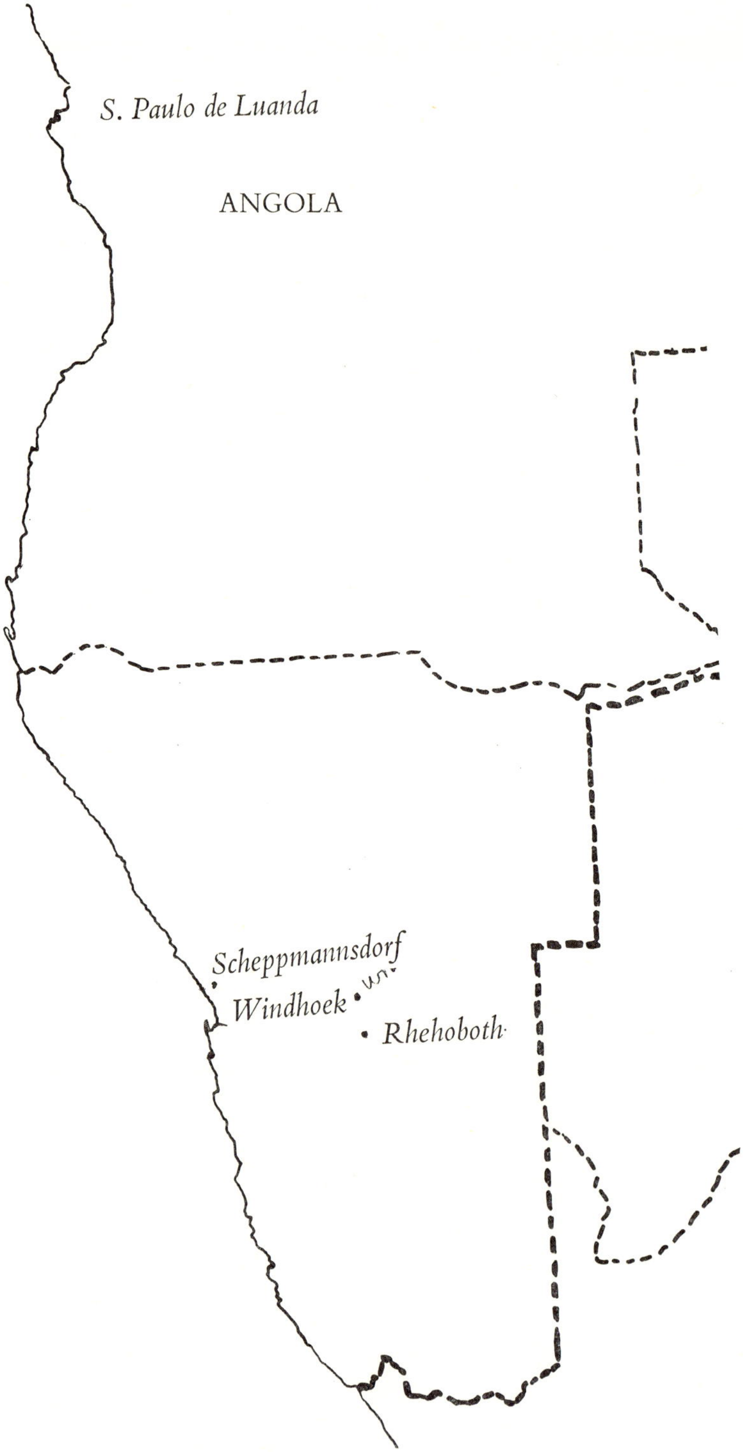
S. Paulo de Luanda
ANGOLA
Scheppmannsdorf
Windhoek
Rhehoboth

start until the middle of the last century. Raul Neves Dias[1] has published a study of the history of the periodical press in Moçambique for the period 1854–1954, on the occasion of a commemorative exhibition in Lourenço Marques to mark the first century of printing in Moçambique. The first item to be printed in Moçambique in the capital city of this name was an official bulletin *(Boletim do Governo da Provincia de Moçambique)* issued on 13 May 1854. The first journal in Lourenço Marques, the later capital of this territory, was published on 15 December 1888 and was entitled *Districto de Lourenço Marques.* The printer was Empreza Typographica Portugueza. No printing seems to have been done in Beira until 1892, when the *Boletim da Companhia de Moçambique* appeared on 1 July. The press was that of the Company.

Filipe Gastão de Almeida de Eça investigated the matter very carefully and in his *Qual foi o Primeiro Livro Impresso em Moçambique?* published in Lisbon in 1953 as a separate of an article from numbers 341–342 of the *Boletim Geral do Ultramar* decided that the *Almanach Civil, Ecclesiastico Historico-Administrativo da Provincia de Moçambique paro o Anno de 1859, 3e depois do Bissexto*, by J. V. da Gama, issued by the Moçambique Imprensa Nacional in 1859, was the first book. So once again, as happens in almost every part of Southern Africa, the first publication is either an almanac or an official gazette.

1. Dias, R. N. *A Imprensa Periodica em Moçambique 1854–1954; coordenacao e notas, etc.* (Lourenço Marques, Imprensa Nacional de Moçambique, printer, 1956).

Military Printing in South Africa

In April 1876 the 'List of Changes in War Material and of Patterns of Military Stores which have been approved and sealed' included under Paragraph 2903 'Wagon, office, without internal fittings, with box complete, suitable for office, telegraph office and printing office (Mark II)'. The Librarian of the War Office kindly made this information available, and stated that 'Wagons, printing' first appear in the 'Priced Vocabulary of Stores used in Her Majesty's service, 1875'. It would appear that this wagon was not used in the field in South Africa before the Bechuanaland Expedition in 1884, when Sir Charles Warren took a force of five thousand men to expel the Boers of Goshen from Bechuanaland.

Section VII of the 'Priced Vocabulary of Stores' issued in 1882 contains a full list of the contents of the printing wagon, and specifically mentions 'Presses, Albion, post folio 1' for which the contract price was £15. Type was carried as follows:

Brevier, roman, caps, lower case, figures, and shilling marks	27 lbs
Great Primer, caps, lower case and figures	15 lbs
Long Primer, complete fount	120 lbs
„ „ italics	14 lbs

The Royal Engineers were in charge of the wagon, and on 18 June 1885 Lt.-Col. A. G. Durnford of the Bechuanaland Field Force reported as follows:

WORK DONE BY PRINTERS

The printing wagon sent out with the Force has proved itself extremely useful.

On the voyage out standing orders for the field force were printed, and a large amount of printing work, including printing the daily general orders and numerous other documents resulting in a great saving of clerical labour, has been very satisfactorily executed.

The non-commissioned officer and men in charge have done their work very well, and the quantity and description of type and other articles supplied have been found to be sufficient.

The wagon itself and its fittings have stood very well the long march up country. The only point which requires improvement is the mode of lighting. The present railway lamps are very unsatisfactory, and their abolition and the substitution of brackets to carry candles is strongly recommended.

A rather similar vehicle was sent, first with the Natal Field Force, and then with Lord Roberts in the South African War of 1899–1902. In such a van[1] the *Ladysmith Lyre* and other siege literature were printed, although its primary object was the printing of military orders, proclamations, etc. W. C. Pocock was in charge of the mobile printing press at Ladysmith, and afterwards was on the works staff of *The Rhodesia Herald* for thirty-two years.[2] The same printing wagon was stationed at Middelburg in the Transvaal towards the end of the South African War, and Mr. O. H. Frewin, the Middelburg printer, recalled having a handbill printed on this press announcing the publication of *The Middelburg Herald*.

After Bloemfontein, Johannesburg, and Pretoria had been occupied, the British Army commandeered one of the local newspaper presses and issued a newspaper of its own during the War of 1899–1902. The most famous of these was *The Friend* in Bloemfontein. Lord Roberts entered the Orange Free State capital on 13 March 1900. Arthur Barlow[3] was not prepared to continue publishing *The Friend*, so the Chief Press Censor, Lord Stanley, arranged with Percival Landon (*The Times* correspondent), H. A. Gwynne (Reuter's chief correspondent), F. W. Buxton (of *The Star*), and Julian Ralph (of the *Daily Mail*, London) to run the paper. Landon telegraphed Rudyard Kipling, then in Cape Town, for a contribution, which he sent. At Lord Roberts's request Kipling joined the staff, and other journalists, such as Lionel James, Bennett Burleigh, A. B. Paterson, and the artist Melton Prior, all contributed. For one month only, 16 March to 16 April 1900, these journalists ran this paper. 'Never again,' said Kipling, 'will there be such a paper. Never again such a staff. Never such fine larks.'[4] Lord Roberts used the newspaper for announcements. So the first page was official; the inner pages contained war news, local gossip, a few overseas cables, and some general reading matter. Kipling also had to select verse suitable for publication from the mass the troops sent in. He so much enjoyed working on this paper that he founded a dining-club, the 'Friendlies', with a badge and a masonic ritual, which survived until Julian Ralph's early death.

1. Wilson, H. W. *After Pretoria, etc.* (London), Amalgamated Press, 1902, vol. 1, p. 164.
2. *The South African Typo Journal*, Apr. 1950, p. 19.
3. *The Friend, 1850–1950: a Century of achievement: special centenary supplement to* The Friend, *June 10, 1950*, p. 11.
4. Carrington, C. *Rudyard Kipling: his Life and Work*. London, Macmillan, 1955, p. 306–308.

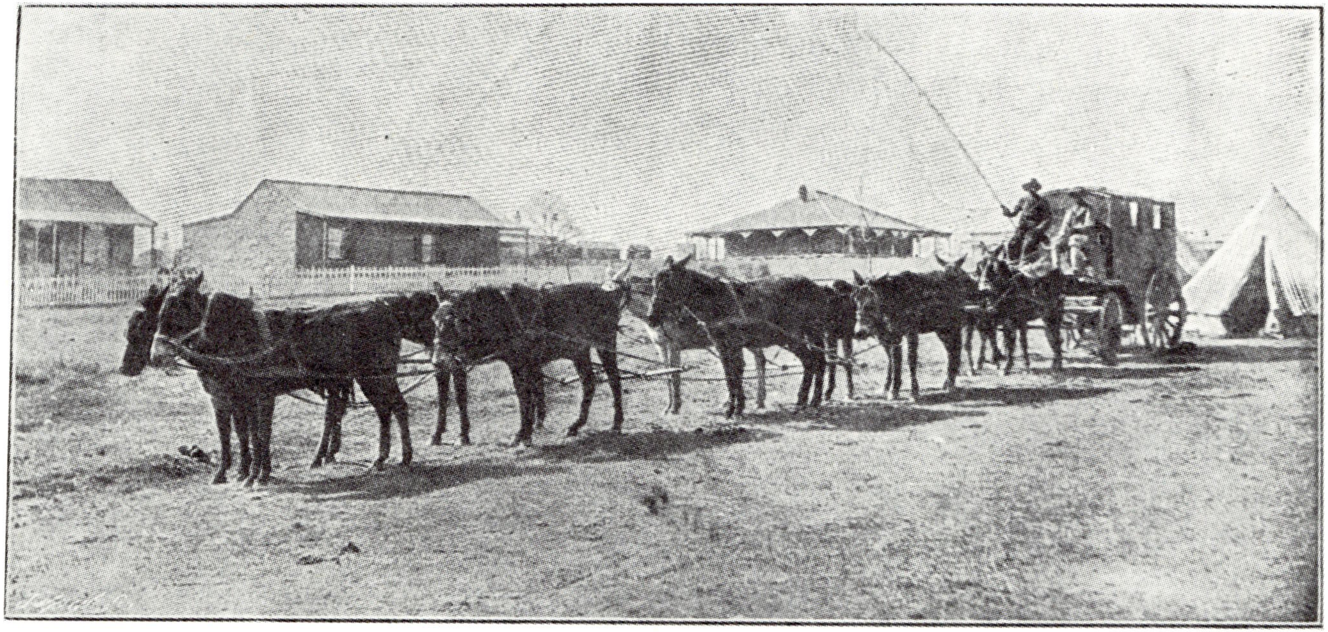

The travelling printing press of the Royal Engineers, housed in a fair-sized wagon, drawn by ten animals (probably mules). The wagon was stored with cases of type and a hand-operated platen press (for an interior view see overleaf). The availability of the press during campaigns constituted a considerable saving of clerical labour as military orders, proclamations etc. could be printed instead of having to be written out by hand. From: H. W. Wilson, After Pretoria, *vol. 1, London 1902.*

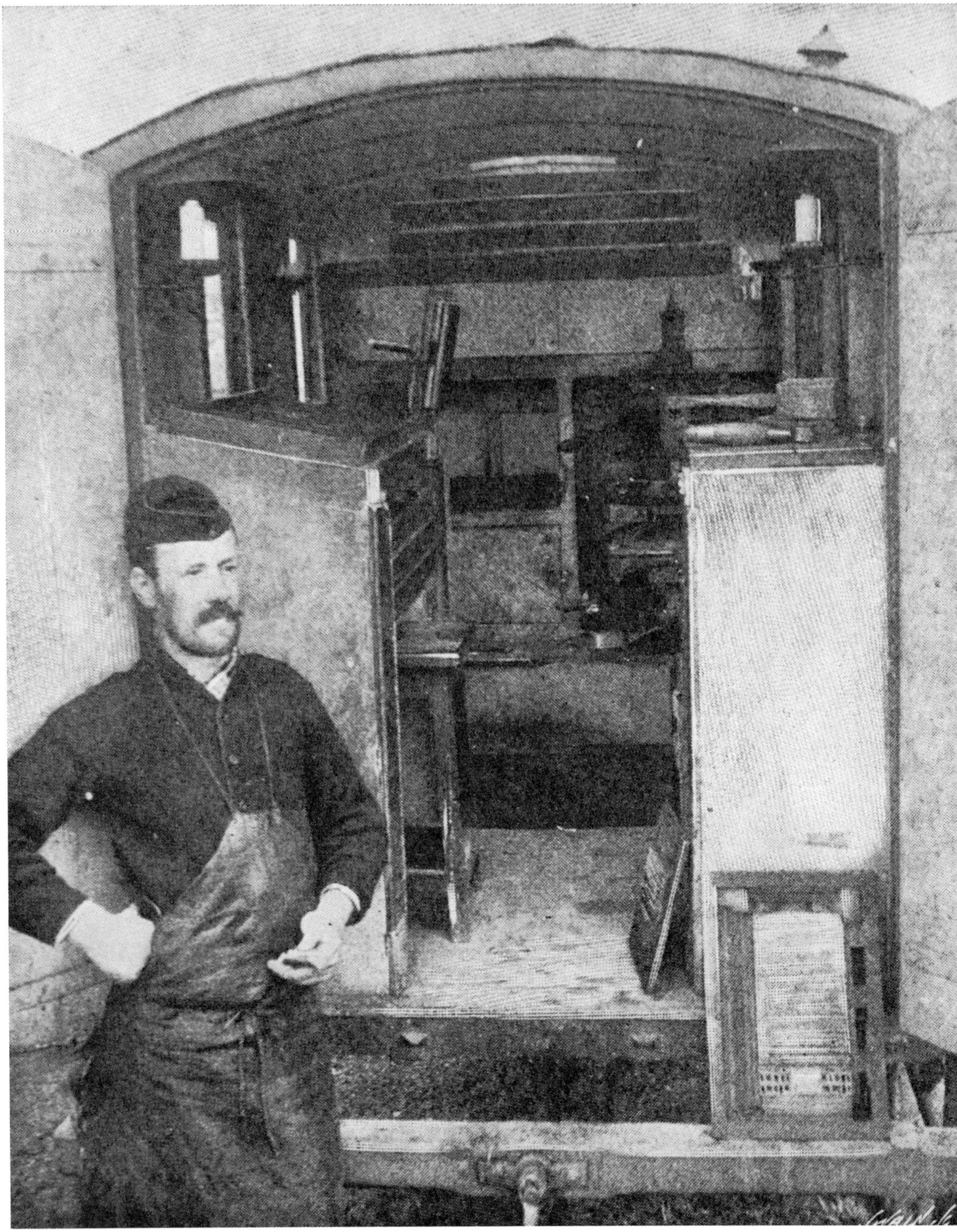

James Barnes,[1] who was also in Bloemfontein at the time tells of his experiences on *The Friend* at this time:

> ... owing to the absence of the correspondents at a little skirmish up the railway line and my being temporarily on the invalid list, it fell upon me to get out the issue of the paper. It was, of all the issues, probably the most remarkable.
>
> When one takes into consideration that any newspaper generally has a staff of assistants—the typographers and pressmen supposed to be at least in accord with the editor and desirous of doing the work—it can be seen that, with only one man to do the proof-reading and composition and also, in this case, to watch a corps of semi-dissatisfied and wholly disaffected compositors, mistakes might occur. The presses were a good three minutes' walk from the editorial sanctum, the means of communication being several small boys impressed for the occasion.
>
> It happened on this day that some news had come through from Cape Town, telling of doings in England—the results of the big horse races—also some rather important news of affairs in China and the East.
>
> It was a splendid opportunity to get out an advance sheet; I hurried to take advantage of it. There are startling headlines! The evening edition was to proclaim 'The Winner of the Lincolnshire,' 'Russia's Fleet off Korea's Coast,' 'The Debate in Parliament,' etc., etc. Altogether I had made up a startling and original 'bill'.
>
> The galley-proofs came back in due form; everything appeared to be going well. But imagine my consternation, when the evening edition appeared, to find that not a line of my much exploited matter appeared in the paper! One page was full of the most ridiculous and distressing typographical errors. There was a story that began in the middle and ended nowhere. Such a hodge-podge of stuff was never before sold by a newsboy; and it all came about thus:
>
> The assistant head of the composing room was a very much unreconstructed Krugerite. The foreman was away, a fact of which I was not aware, and the unreconstructed one had taken advantage of the moment and the absence of the regular editors to have a little fun on his own account; aided by a bottle of Dop brandy, he had it! Strange to say, the good-natured people who had paid a penny for the paper did not raid the offices. The whole thing was set down as a hoax on the part of the management. Although the real news appeared on the following day, and the jocose printer was relieved of further participation in the typesetting department, I was regarded as a humorist.

In Johannesburg the plant of *The Standard and Diggers' News* was commandeered after the British had taken the town on 31 May 1900, and from 2 June 1900 *The Johannesburg Gazette* was printed. All military notices were published in this journal.[2]

Between 26 June and 14 July 1900 when the British first occupied Pretoria, they published their military proclamations and notices, and a few items of news in a

1. Barnes, J. *From Then till Now: Anecdotal Portraits and Transcript Pages from Memory's Tablets, etc.* New York, D. Appleton-Century, 1934, p. 287–288.
2. Bell, W. H. S. *Bygone Days, etc.* London, H. & F. Witherby, (1933), p. 137.

journal called the *Pretoria Friend*, which the military established for this purpose.

The *Mafeking Mail* was established on 20 May 1899 as a weekly. Between November 1899 and May 1900, shells permitting, it went on appearing all through the siege on all kinds and colours of paper. The issues for this period are known as the 'Siege Slips' and are greatly treasured. What is usually seen is a reprint of the full set issued shortly after the siege by Townshend & Son, the firm responsible for printing under fire. The bound volume contains a special preface by the editor, G. N. H. Whales. The *Mafeking Mail* became a daily in September 1900.

The Boers also had presses in the field. The *Volkstem* was at Elandslaagte with a small hand press, and editions were also printed at Glencoe and Kroonstad.[1] Unfortunately very few indeed of these field issues have survived. A special daily edition with war news was published in Pretoria until the British entered the city in June 1900. The *African Review* of 9 December 1899 informed its readers as follows:

> The Volksstem, Dr. Leyds's organ at Pretoria, has a travelling printing press, with a full equipment of compositors, etc. at the front in General Joubert's chief laager. The printing apparatus is fixed in a roomy railway carriage, which has attached to it another carriage fitted up as an editor's & reporter's room.

F. J. Wulfse, who was born in Dordrecht in Holland in 1875, and was apprenticed to *The Press* in Pretoria in 1888, before serving in the Staatsdrukkery, wrote to *Die Vaderland* in Johannesburg on 1 October 1946 to say that after Bloemfontein had fallen into British hands, President Steyn asked President Kruger to send a field printing press to the Free State. A railway coach was fitted as a printing works. Mr. Wulfse was the compositor, Ben Wallach the pressman and a Mr. Morgenroodt and a Mr. te Groen made up the complement of the staff. The coach was standing at Kroonstad to start with, but was finally forced to move to Germiston. At this time Lord Roberts was entering Johannesburg, so when Mr. Wulfse tried to return from the Johannesburg suburb of Braamfontein, where he had been to see his betrothed, the railway coach had left for Waterval Boven, and he never saw it again.

In the South African Public Library, Cape Town, there is a manifesto of 30 pages in Dutch by P. B. Walters dated June 1901 bearing the imprint 'Gedrukt door de Veld-drukkery van de Regering der Z.A.R.' (Printed by the Field press of the Government of the South African Republic).

1. Nienaber, P. J. *'n Beknopte Geskiedenis van die Hollands-Afrikaanse Drukpers in Suid-Afrika*. Kaapstad, Nasionale Pers, 1943, p. 101.

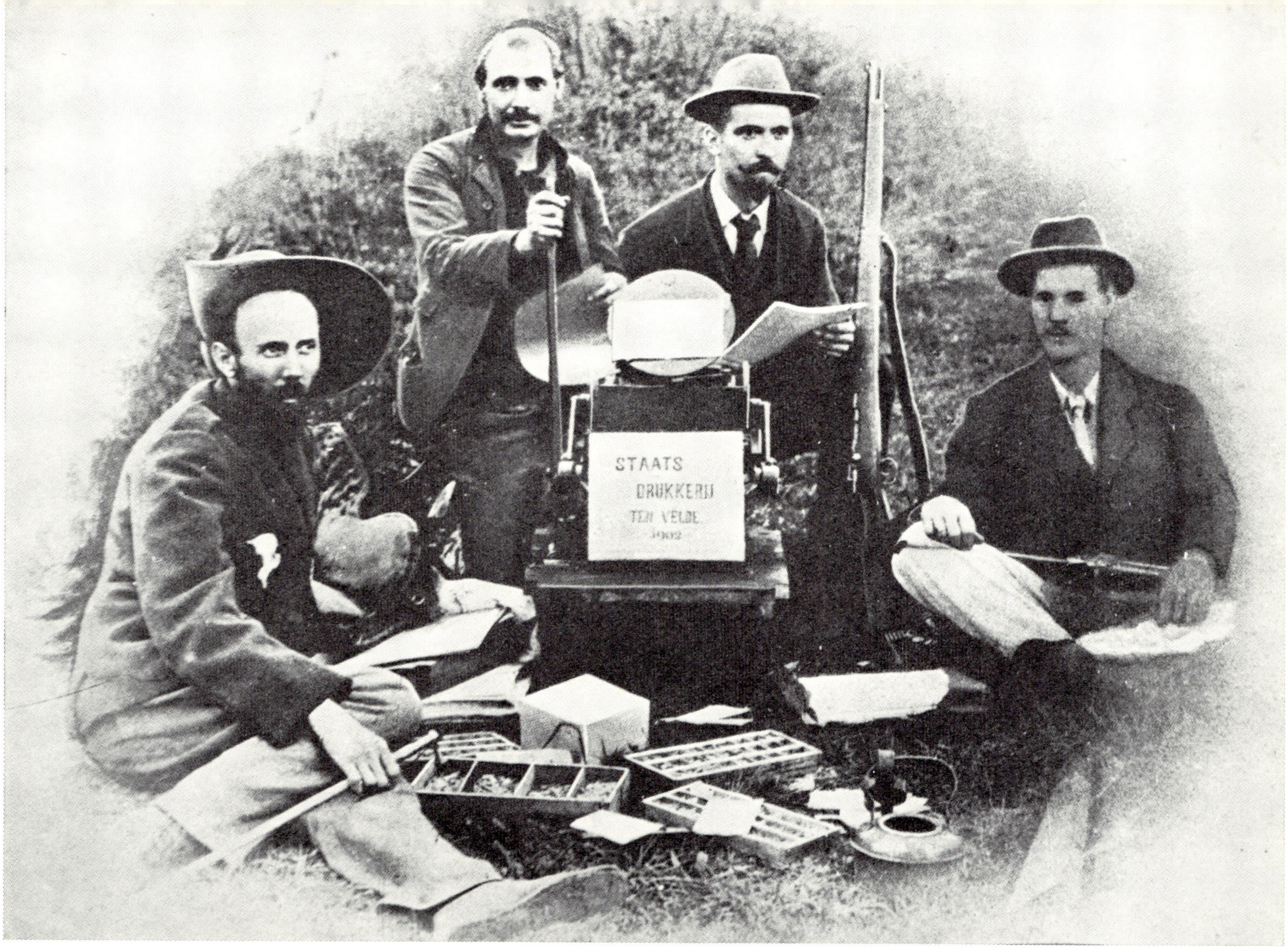

The staff of the field press of the Zuid-Afrikaansche Republiek in 1902. It seems unlikely that the few cases of type and the small hand-operated platen press constituted the whole of their equipment; but as we do not know exactly where and when the photograph was taken (obviously in the final stages of the war) more facts cannot be ascertained. From: A. Marshall, Photos of the Boer Commandos.

The Johannesburg paper, *The Transvaal Leader* of 14 March 1911, published the following:

DE WET'S PRINTING PRESS

When leaving Kroonstad, the members of the Free State Government took with them a small printing press for the printing of official notices, which had originally been used by the Railway Department. This press accompanied the peripatetic Government in all its retreats on fresh 'capitals'. Eventually it was left at Fouriesburg, where the Ficksburg men, after their wanderings, set it up again when they retired to the place. Mr. Mels Meyers was at that time acting as Vrederechter in Fouriesburg, and was told that a printing press and its complement had been found in one of the houses. It was the press which had been with President Steyn and General De Wet, and which had been abandoned when it could no longer be 'retired' to them. Mr. Meyers learned to set the type and use the press, and the latter throughout the exciting times of the following month turned out official forms, Christmas cards, and the commando periodical 'De Brandwag'. It was hidden at times in a kloof. When Fouriesburg was evacuated by the burger forces in April, 1900, the press had to be left behind in the flight, but it was rescued on a wagon a few days later, though the rescuers were subsequently pursued by soldiers. Some time subsequently Meyers was captured while with Kritzinger, in the Cape Colony, the press having previously been handed over to someone else.

What happened to the press afterwards is not known, but it is on record that the *Government Gazette* of the Orange Free State was printed at Fouriesburg,[1] presumably on this press.

Some twenty different special wartime journals of the South African War period are known. The British publications are either regimental journals or siege issues: the Boers generally wrote theirs to while away the time in prisoner-of-war camps in various parts of the world. Only very occasionally were any of these journals printed. Consequently most are outside the scope of the present survey.

There have not been many garrison presses in South Africa, but there was one at Grahamstown and later at Keiskamma Hoek in the early 'sixties (where some issues of the *North Lincoln Sphinx* were printed for the Tenth Regiment), and the South African Constabulary is thought to have had a press in Bloemfontein at the old fort on Monument Hill towards the end of the South African War.

At the time of the South African War it is clear that printing was going on throughout Southern Africa. Most of the technical inventions and improvements

1. Cutten, T. E. G. *A History of the Press in South Africa, etc.* Cape Town, National Union of South African Students, 1935, p. 68.

made in Europe to printing machinery throughout the century had penetrated at least to the bigger centres, where most types of printing could be performed. The quality, however, was generally speaking poor, and no single press was noted for fine printing. Strange to say, although South African printing throughout the century was greatly influenced by Britain from which, with a few exceptions, its printing materials and imported printers came, the British reaction to the degeneration of the art of printing shown mainly in the publications inspired by William Morris, had, by the end of the century, not affected South African work. South African authors had at this time not yet become accustomed to having their books locally printed, and the printers themselves inevitably were inexperienced in the making of books. All this was to change in time, and the first signs of these changes came immediately after the South African War, which can therefore be looked upon as the end of an era in the history of South African printing.

Some Basic Works

Bosman, F. C. L. *Hollandse Joernalistiek in Suid-Afrika gedurende die 19de Eeu, etc.* (Kaapstad, Federale Drukpers Maats.), [1930?].

Botha, C. G. 'Geskiedenis van die drukpers in Suid-Afrika' in *Die Huisgenoot*, February 1921, p. 4114.

Cutten, T. E. G. *A History of the Press in South Africa, etc.* Cape Town, National Union of South African Students, 1935.

Dias, R. N. *A Imprensa Periodica em Moçambique 1854–1954: coordenação e notas, etc.* (Lourenço Marques, Imprensa nacional de Moçambique, printer, 1956).

Jenkins, O. 'Our Prnting Pioneers' in *The South African Printer and Stationer*, December 1939, p. 361.

Laidler, P. W. *The Pre-Victorian Products of the Cape Press.* Johannesburg, no pub., 1935. (South African Library Association Bibliography, No. 1.)

Meurant, L. H. *Sixty Years ago: or, Reminiscences of the Struggle for the Freedom of the Press in South Africa, etc.* Cape Town, Saul Solomon, 1885.

Morrison, W. R. *A Brief History of South African Printing... and Catalogue of Exhibition of Early South African Printing.* [Johannesburg?] no pub., [1934?].

Nienaber, P. J. *'n Beknopte Geskiedenis van die Hollands-Afrikaanse Drukpers in Suid-Afrika.* Kaapstad, Nasionale Pers, 1943.

Robinson, A. M. Lewin. *None daring to make us afraid, etc.* Cape Town, Maskew Miller, 1962.

Rosenthal, E. *160 Years of Cape Town Printing.* (Cape Town, Cape Town Association of Printing House Craftsmen and the Cape Chamber of Printing, 1960).

Smith, Anna H. 'Chronological List of the More Important Places in South Africa where Printing was introduced during the Early Years' in *South African Libraries*, vol. 6, No. 2, Oct. 1938, p. 67–71, with map.

South Africa in Print: Catalogue of an Exhibition of Books, Atlases and Maps held in the

South African Library Cape Town, 1 March till 5 April 1952 in Commemoration of the arrival of Jan van Riebeeck at the Cape 6 April 1652. Cape Town, Book Exhibition Committee Van Riebeeck Festival, 1952.

Today's News Today: the story of the Argus Company. Johannesburg, Argus Printing and Publishing Co., (1956).

Varley, D. H. 'An early Cape Printing Discovery' in *Quarterly Bulletin of the South African Library*, v.l, No. 1, Dec. 1946, p. 3–8.

Venter, I. S. J. 'Die Rol van die Drukpers in die Wesleyaanse Betsjoeana sending gedurende die Halfeeu 1825–1875' in *Historia*, September 1955, p. 162.

Index